CONTENT

Dear readers, we always want to support you and give you the information you need to have the best reading experience possible. Please note that Lit Shark's Best Of 2023 Anthology contains content pertaining to mental health, child loss, cancer diagnoses and treatments, animal death, broken hearts, and tremendous examples of grief. There are also multiple illusions to sexual activity and some use of expletives. Thank you again for your support. We hope you will enjoy our inaugural anthology!

COPYRIGHT

Editor-in-Chief: McKenzie Lynn Tozan
Book Cover and Interior Design: McKenzie Lynn Tozan
Works By: Various Writers (credited)
Cover Image By: Open Source, Anonymous
Cover Spine Image By: Slaveika Aladjova
First Edition 2024

LITERARY ANTHOLOGY · ISSUES NO. 1-4 · 2024

LIT SHARK
magazine

THE **BEST OF 2023** ANTHOLOGY

EDITED BY MCKENZIE LYNN TOZAN

SOMETHING OLD, SOMETHING NEW
SOMETHING TO SINK YOUR TEETH INTO

LETTER FROM THE EDITOR

Hi readers, writers, and shark fans!

True to every new year, I feel like January and February flew by, and I'm still reeling from all that happened in 2023 while I'm trying to find my footing in the new year. But at least this year, I'm saying that in a good way.

Though I first thought of Lit Shark Magazine and what I hoped it could be clear back in 2015, 2023 was the year of its actual launch—and it's already been so much more than I originally expected it would be. The response has been lovely, supportive, and the excitement has been contagious. I'm so grateful.

I've been so pleased throughout 2023 and the earliest parts of 2024 to see how writers broach and make new common subjects like love, family, and identity, and I've been especially interested in seeing how nature interweaves with those themes, especially marine life, birds, coral, and echolocation. I've always loved nature writing, particularly nonfiction and ecopoetics, and the work that has come through Lit Shark has made these subjects feel like living, breathing entities to me—because in so many ways, they are.

To celebrate, I wanted to do something that would offer a shoutout to all of the wonderful people I worked with this year, all they contributed, and what they've gone on to do beyond Lit Shark, as well. Enter: Lit Shark's *Best Of 2023 Anthology*.

Lit Shark received over 1,200 unique submissions in 2023, and just under 300 of those pieces were accepted in Issues 1 through 4. That doesn't include the submissions we received for our Poem of the Month contest in October, November, and December, either! Submissions have already started to come in for 2024, and I can't wait to see how big we can go this year.

For our inaugural Best Of anthology, we revisited all of our issues—Issue One, Issue Two: The SHARK WEEK Edition, Issue Three: The Spooky (TEETH) Edition, and Issue Four—and selected our 50 favorite pieces by 50 writers. We then invited each of those 50 writers to submit something new that we could include in the anthology, resulting in a "something old and something new, something to sink your teeth into" collection that we love. It was fascinating to see how these "old and new" pieces spoke to each other, even when they were observing different themes!

The anthology is organized into three sections—Poetry, Prose (fiction and nonfiction), and the Poem of the Month winners and honorable mentions for the year—and you'll see the writer's "old" piece positioned first, followed by their "new" piece. In a few cases, you'll see a piece "out of genre," because the writer previously published a poem and submitted a story as their "new" piece, or vice versa.

Looking back over this anthology, these pieces carry with them an irrevocable focus on love, loss, and grief. Before reading this collection in its entirety, I never realized how beautifully, perfectly, bittersweetly, and heartbreakingly the metaphor of drowning, water, and the murky depths are to the grieving process, and how endless and impossible that phase of life can be. Perhaps it's a reflection of things going on in my own life, why I chose these pieces and how they fit so wonderfully together, but I hope this collection proves to not just be a beautiful example of poetry and story for you, but also an object of comfort like it's turning out to be for me.

I really hope you enjoy this collection and give yourself the time to simply sit back and relax in it. Maybe it's because I've been so close to these pieces all year long, but when I read this collection, I can feel Lit Shark's growth in it; I can feel the swell of excitement and anticipation; and I can feel this urgency for what is to come. Maybe it's just me, but I hope you will feel it, too.

Thank you again for all of the support you've shown Lit Shark in the past year. I cannot wait to see what is to come in 2024, and I'm honored to have you along for the ride with me.

In Celebration,
McKenzie
Editor-in-Chief and Fellow Shark Fan
March 2024

CONTENTS

PROSE

2023 POEM OF THE MONTH

POETRY

GLEN ARMSTRONG

SHARK WEEK

We settle in for shark.
Week.
T.S. Eliot would have no.
Doubt done the same.
There's a name for what we feel.
When we see that mouth.
Alien and deadly.
Twisting through waters.
That twist through the world.
We settle for.

These images on a screen.
While something preexists.
Defying its name.
And its offspring and its appetite.
We hold hands and dim the lights.
We readjust our bodies.
And wonder what will happen next.
We have never been.
To the ocean.
This is how the world begins.

GLEN ARMSTRONG

FURTHER PREDICTIONS

This year *pair* magically.
Transforms from a noun to a verb.
It will be all about the doing.
And less so that which does.
Leave bees and lesser drunks.
To the sounds they make.
You will enjoy the scenic landscape.
Both literally and figuratively.
So will I.
A wild boar will visit.

The adjacent neighborhood.
It's all well and good.
To embrace.
That which has yet to come.
Snooping about for truffles or trash.
In sharp contrast *laugh*.
Will transition from verb to noun.
Decline all invitations to go.
Out for a few of them.
This new laugh will bare its teeth.

KB BALLENTINE

BLUE PERSISTENCE

Wave pursues wave, and wind spirals,
lashing hair across my face.
One, two, no, three vessels linger on the horizon,
seeming specks in spite of their large truth.
Sand gives way to pebbles and sheared shells –
foam skittering toward the dunes.
Spray stains my legs as peach, then a searing
orange, purges twilight's remains
Farther down the shore, a man wobbles
in a shuffling run, a woman throws a ball
for her collie. But they are far from me.
Here I have the sandpipers rushing my feet,
the gulls screaming overhead.
                              You in my heart.

KB BALLENTINE

HOPE

Whitecaps foam and leap
   the surface of the sea,
     toss like horses their wild
   manes of waves and spray.
What am I waiting for
   here on this spit of land?
This little bit of sand and shingle
   where one more step
     would take my breath away?
   Scoured by salt, by wind—
the stones, my face glisten.
   Wildness brings its own beauty,
like silvery salmon winding
     toward the mouth of home.
Even the Memory beyond memories—
   that Other place doesn't sting,
doesn't surge but settles into the depths
     of our souls where longing lives.
   It dances in that place—waiting
for our return.

JANET BOWDAN

LANDBANK, NANTUCKET

When you walk the loop, which we do
despite wanting that sight of beach
because the ocean is three miles and another three
back and among us we have a bad knee,
a problem foot, and an 8-year-old who has two
gears—dawdle and run—you take a path
through fields occasionally mowed so
they'll look like they did when they were farmed
cooperatively; you pass high bush blueberries in
bloom and black cherry trees and trees webbed
with caterpillar larvae just beginning to emerge
so it looks a bit like Mirkwood except open to the sun.
But everywhere you hear birds, even if you don't
see them, and then you come across the high pole
with the osprey nest, and the osprey takes off,
opening her wings to the breeze, calling.
There is a kettle pool 15,000 years old and a sign that this
is the last of the glacial moraine that came just
this far south on Nantucket. Martha's Vineyard,
next island over, is eroding at such a rate that they're
slowly moving the Gay Point Lighthouse 134 feet back
from the cliff side. Signs for the Land Bank
don't explain how this works, only that it's here:
a public trust. We have to live on the interest, so
we need to make regular deposits, keep an eye on
our investments, save, preserve, stockpile these lands.
Our way of saving something as the jade-green ocean
batters fiercely, constantly at the edges of the shores.

JANET BOWDAN

PLACES WE ARE NEVER GOING

Let's start with the one where the spiders are so big
they eat birds. Not happening, no matter how highly
recommended. Nor are we going back to high school
which, I don't care how long it's been, some people
never grow up, as manifested by the two events planned:
open bar and pig roast. Do you know, I managed
to avoid that high school's town for 20 years
even though it's right next to the one I live in now?
If it hadn't been for the bike path, I would have made it
to 25 years. But Blair bought me the bike,
we weren't even married yet, and kissed me
on the bike path, his hooked-in-bike shoes nearly
cascading him and me and all four wheels onto the ground.
And just before our wedding a few weeks later,
biking past the school reunion, he yelled from the path,
"I got the Valedictorian!" Was there a fuck you in there?
It was an implied fuck you, if not his, mine, yes,
the Valedictorian's, who, for her grand award, got
a dictionary, as if someone who's top of her class
wouldn't already have a dictionary, even an OED.
Nobody said I couldn't hold grudges like a Valedictorian.
And okay, it's been years. It's been so long,
but two years ago we were biking on that path,
got almost to the end when there, at the end,
a large black bear emerged from the shrubs and
we're no fools: we just turned those bikes around
and headed home.

CATHERINE BROADWALL

APPRAISAL

Thumbing through an old diary,
I come upon the question: *Is grief*

a measure of goodness? The query
sucks my ribs in tight, and I

wonder: the value of the rubies
of grieving that drip from

my fingers in ropes. Reading on,
I see I meant funerals, the grieving

of a person that takes place
in their wake. *Is the grief poured*

over a person a measure of their
goodness? is what I meant.

But I like this other reading,
the question it poses: could all this

grief mean goodness? Refusal
to drown out the pet's shocking

death? Refusal to shut out the
world and its roiling, ever-present

loss? I imagine placing it on a
scale, this pocketful of grief

gems. Having some appraiser
raise it to her eye, say, *Don't you know*

what this is worth?! Like those
episodes where someone's thrift

store painting is a long-lost
masterpiece. I know this likely isn't

how God works, but
what a downy thought.

That an appraiser might gather
up all this blood and say,

Congratulations.
You kept your heart soft.

CATHERINE BROADWALL

VILLANELLE WITH ANXIETY AS BANSHEE

Through the mist she pursues me, her mouth full of screams.
With eyes red from crying, and wringing of hands,
She pulls at the night sky, unstitching its seams.

The bolt of her sorrow unfurls in reams.
She paces along the glow of the sands.
Through the mist she pursues me, her mouth full of screams.

Her tangled hair billows wherever wind deems.
She's followed for days, all over these lands.
She pulls at the night sky, unstitching its seams.

If I slump into slumber, she's there in my dreams,
seething that no one ever understands.
Through the mist she pursues me, her mouth full of screams.

Though the sun has come up, clouds cover its beams.
As it sinks behind mountains, she issues demands.
She pulls at the night sky, unstitching its seams.

The moonlight is sallow, a mess of blurred creams.
Her grip on my wrists leaves a pair of tight bands.
Through the mist she pursues me, her mouth full of screams.
She pulls at the night sky, unstitching its seams.

LORRAINE CAPUTO

MEDITATION: GALÁPAGOS SEAS

Surrounded by
      shattered coral
      & sea-burnished lava
I sit in the warm
      late-afternoon sun
      listening
to the tide rising, waves
      leaping over fractured
      boulders, waves rising
translucent green-blue
      to break, frothing, arriving
      to shore, before
relaxing

Red crabs cling
      to those black crags,
      the serge breaking &
      foaming over them
& out yonder
      two boobies skim
      the waters, back & forth
      along this ragged coast
one flies near, its
      turquoise feet tucked
      against its white belly

LORRAINE CAPUTO

WASHED

This near-full moon's light
slithers through the broken clouds,

across this sea's gentle waves
washing upon the fine sands,

a soft whisper ebbing & flowing,
sea froth phosphorescent

beneath the luna's pearly beams,
leaving wavering prints upon the strand . . .

I lay upon the beach, gazing upon that moon
& yonder points of shimmering lights,

these stars strewn across the deep blue velvet heaven . . .
a song rising to my lips, a humming

punctuated by those waves' lapping,
licking the bottoms of my bare feet, refreshing them,

tingling with the desire to walk many-a mile,
my prints washed away.

ALAN COHEN

VISIT

The past has habits
Has, like the hummingbird
Been away awhile
But now, just when you are crazy busy
Hums a few bars
And, hovering suddenly in memory
Seems as close as sometimes
The perfect word, the right job
Heaven; then, as you grow accustomed
Begin to measure
The ruby on its throat
It shifts, hovers askance
Owing you nothing
And is gone again
It may be for weeks, forever
No more yours, what you saw
And said and did
Than your house or your car
Or your life
Things you have for a time
That lose something
When they lose you
But go on

ALAN COHEN

AFTERMATH

The caress of summer
After a bleak, pluvial spring
Came like mastery after illness
For a few vivid hours
We felt reborn
In greenness and sunlight and promise

How often in the aftermath of storms
As we've turned a new historical page
Have we not tried, in the gladsome hush
To draw a prudent balance between greed and acquiescence
Love and freedom

After each failure
The new storms have been more intense
Perhaps then history is linear, fraught
Has no arc, cannot bend
Just one day, gone brittle with use, will break, end

MARK CONNORS

FORCE

There is water
cascading down
from rock it has
smoothed, gushing
forth in that masculine
way water does.
You are beneath,
edging ever closer,
aware it can sink you,
hold you in place
till you drown.
It's for sale now.
you can buy it,
and the ancient
wood whose
inhabitants listen
to its music,
aware of the trace
of a teenage boy
who the water
sunk and held fast
two summers back.
You can't help
remember him
the moment
you feel spray
on your face,
how close you are
to turning back
for the safely
of the shale bed.

MARK CONNORS

LOOKING UP

Don't look for meaning from the corvids
on the towpath. There's more to life

than joy and sorrow, no matter how many magpies
caw at us. Ask anyone who has given birth.

They get it wrong all the time.

No. Look to the sky. Read it like
a weather man, a weather woman,

or however you choose to identify.
Breathe. We all need omens on our side.

DALE E. COTTINGHAM

STOP LIGHT

I waited my turn. Will I proceed
in the old way, the one that's given,
that's easy, worn smooth, or will I
take another, rougher, more
against-the-grain road
into the lowlands,
who will I be . . .

Soon enough I'll go on. There'll be
temptations, signs to interpret,
choices between self and others.
I'll be influenced. I'll be right, I'll
be wrong. I'll try to get a glimpse
through the fog. And looking
back it will seem like a weave,
one thing connected to another,
like a journey one is on,
like a poem,
like song.

DALE E. COTTINGHAM

QUIBBLE

About need, do I
have a choice? Wind
drives clouds to
all manner of places.

I am like the clouds,
riding on currents
of hunger, lust, greed,
sometimes mixed together.

There's an instinct
that seldom occurs in humans,
but I've seen it,
to deny oneself,

the ones who
give what little
they have—it could be
any hour,

unremarkable,
not realizing the
sign they make when
they put others first—

to me a great strength
but to others
a weakness
as they turn

to the work
they will expend
themselves in
and make a forgettable name.

I turn everywhere.
I see shapes by which
a quibble declares itself,
made more acute

by those voices
that pronounce
that self-expression
is what we're born for,

the face, for example,
in a glow of neon light,
that focuses: you see
the eyes,

that appear searching,
with a searcher's tendency
to make herself appear lonelier,
then alone. I'm not reckless.

I know I have needs.
In dream I get
to make up things as they go,
who to sit with, where we go after,

with all the precious freight of dreams,
but need, relentless, roving,
a steel chord,
knows what it wants.

PATRICK DRUGGAN

SHEARWATER

We stand on the beach, an August storm
is gathering over Wales, dark as rage.

We can't stay long.
It will rain soon.

Waves, waves, the children,
of the unseen Moon and wind

Suddenly,
the water rises up
and crashes
as the world takes its toll

His hands flutter by his eyes
flocks of shearwaters
among the waves
as he amazes at the chaos in the foam

He pulls his hair.
I don't know why.
I never do.
Some hidden
unseen effect
of space
and time
his capacity,
to cope, eroded

My mind tenses.
My body stiffens,
against his wind.

Large drops,
Enough change
to distract him,
Tears camouflaged in the sand
as the rain breaks.

PATRICK DRUGGAN

SMIDDY

—for James Smith, 1963 to 2021

I still see him drinking waater
oot a ginger boattle at oor steps.
Charlie says a joke and waater
seems to burst out all the holes in his heid
spraying an aerosol directly at the sun
as he laughs uncontrollably.
His explosion forms a rainbow
his wonder is uncontainable.

I've been taught that a spectrum will form
by the double reflection of light through
the water droplets by diffraction,
—I am unsurprised.

I have knowledge, he has delight
and creates his rainbow five times
in succession, no apology for his joy
at his ability to possess these moments
and live them like a summer day.

With each funeral these memories fade.
I can't make Smiddy's. He died in the village.
Raised his kids in our streets,
Remembering him, I wonder whether
with all my education, all my travel,
I gained less than he was born with.

CAROL EDWARDS

DRIFTWOOD DRYAD

I hold the sky and see in my hands,
feel the heartbeat of Earth in sands.
I hear the song of your raging,
bend to the power of your wind,
my skin scraped clean,
my green
long since dimmed.
Your salt spray scours my bones,
twisted, gnarled, stripped;
beautiful I am not,
save on nights
when I and my sisters tripped
whispered steps in silv'ry light
your waves glimmering,
gossamer veils both gowns and shrouds,
stone-pale tresses billowed crowns
until daybreak, when the spell drowns.

CAROL EDWARDS

TELL ME THE STORY OF THE SLEEPING BEAUTIES WAKED BY TORRENTS OF TEARS:

weeping blue canvas
dissolves diamonds in parched tongues,

small beating hearts push
past their sealed walls, delicate

light weaves an ocean
soft thunders drawing golden,

Earth opens her mouth
downy fluff dancing on breath,

the impulse to leap
shatters mirrors to pieces,

      where brushes stroke air
      strings hunger for hope,

      treasures from their sleep
      spread wishes in white

      far below mists.

MICHAEL FLANAGAN

"SUNLIGHT / ON OLD SNOW"

sunlight
on old snow
pause
snap a picture
in my mind

aha
I finally see that feeling sorry for yourself
is different than grief
now I can see
a light in the darkness

soda bread
so simple a recipe
what could go wrong
then I found out
a lot

MICHAEL FLANAGAN

"LEFT TO RIGHT"

left to right
west to east
the clouds
scuttle
     like
          feathers
    fluttering
to earth

"A GOOD DEED"

a good deed
freeing the wasp caught
in the window screen
then not panicking
as she crawled up my arm

ANNETTE GAGLIARDI

SUSPENSION

The space between
you and me
vibrates;

dawn's burnished
light exhales from
somewhere close.

I smell roses—
the air's caress
that announces the sun

with a clear, high C
that floats through
the garden—and we

take flight,
that same moment
the sun slips into view;

our wings spread
to lift us skyward.

ANNETTE GAGLIARDI

DEEP SIGHS

You pursue
the rhythm of days
spent cohabitating illness,

under cover of carefully
crafted chaos,
returned from neverland

and what you thought
you knew.
Your bones & your flesh —

red and white roses,
to the new order of you,
who are not the same,

yet the resemblance
remains, in your
deepening sighs.

J.D. GEVRY

ALL THAT CAN'T BE SAID

It hung there, in the humid air
adhered to every vaporized droplet:
 Magnetism
 Attachment
 Intimacy
 Love.

We circled each other in silence—
sharks surrounding prey we couldn't
see, but could
 smell
through the waves

Sullen, adrift, searching
for a voice to carry our song
for relief from the tension we couldn't
 name
  but had known her whole life
for a way to hold each other tightly
 under the riptide of our guilt

J.D. GEVRY

TENSION IN THE STITCH

When I consider breaking
us apart, I   tear away from you; inevitably
stitched back   from inside out
ending in a tiny knot   you depend on
see I'm that
specter of a hole you had at the
strained bottom
of your right pocket; all your
change   falling through
black sweatpants I mended for you
pulling a resistant needle
by chipped teeth;   creaky hands
I patched your frayed gap
with Halloween fabric, inside—
a white-glitter skull
no one could see; this
      memento you'll lose, then re-find
remembering it's there   then
remembering   I'm here
as you search for a lighter or
      jingle coins impatiently
in a crowded check-out line
feeling the seam slowly rip
open again
with time
with weight
with wear

GTIMOTHY GORDON

L'AUBE SONG

— Monsoon Season
(September-October 2022)

Hiking in from pour-black-night
owning the heavens before melding
into ether, before I reach desert ridge
at Coyote Springs, Boulders' Green,
exotic dank, musty orange blossom and iris,
snake molt, fresh scat cellar smell,
before first light-strike-glow through Organ Notch,
the coming-in black as the going-out,
as in a dream, spent, yet again,
wet with wonder, clutching nothing
but dawn, before all-blue-clear.

GTIMOTHY GORDON

FOGGED

Mountain fogged
mothball cloud
wrapped in night
even when backlit
by starlight
as all are, earthward,
ground under heaven,
the lame and the halt,
upright, unjust,
watchful, waiting,
even sleepful,
dreaming a clearing come.

SHANNON FROST GREENSTEIN

HEAVY SPOT

Anyone who was anyone –
within the nascent adolescent ranks of elite USA Gymnastics, that is –
went to Camp Woodward.

A co-ed camp for extreme sports,
I remember shyly ogling BMX riders and pierced skater bois.
It turns out a twelve year-old gymnast is no different than any other
      twelve year-old girl;
it turns out the appeal of summer camp is still summer love.

But every year, under the guise of seasonal fun, child athletes worked
      to the bone,
the hiking and color wars which symbolize typical overnight camp
swapped out for early-morning conditioning and two-a-day trainings.

We learned quickly what was expected of our bodies
during this respite from the demands of the school year;
we learned quickly that fear has no place at Camp Woodward.

We learned not to ask for a heavy spot.

To develop muscle memory, a heavy spot is a solace;
in the face of nerves and bodily injury, a heavy spot makes you
      less afraid.
But USA Gymnastics has never paid mind to its athletes' qualms
and USA gymnasts do not require heavy spots.

"HEAVY SPOT!" would echo through the gymnasium –
when a child risking death made the mistake of requesting extra help –

and the entire staff would descend in a flurry,
dozens of coaches rushing to cartoonishly assist with the flip or
    the twist,
hundreds of eyes upon the poor girl who simply wants to keep her
    spinal cord intact;
and everywhere the unspoken assumption
that she is *just not strong enough* to be a gymnast.

I learned at summer camp that asking for help is weakness;
I learned at summer camp to be embarrassed by my own needs.

How often in life, thirty years removed from Camp Woodward,
do I still need a heavy spot?
How often in life, after a lifetime with USA Gymnastics,
do I still abstain from requesting one?

Because I am still embarrassed to vocalize when I am scared;
I still think twice before publicly asking for help.
Art imitates life imitates art, and what is so goddamn wrong
with needing an extra hand in this world?

ALYSSA HARMON

52 BLUE

when someone asks you what
mental illness feels like
tell them that
the 52-hertz whale
is the only one of his species that
has a cry that is too high of a pitch
for other whales to hear,
so he travels alone.

ALYSSA HARMON

THE KIND OF BLUE

have you ever noticed how the sky is
an even more beautiful blue
the day after a storm?
no clouds, just a blue
that begs for attention,
the kind of blue that reminds you why
you keep trying,
the kind of blue that promises to love you
forever, even on your dark purple days,
the kind of blue that holds your hair back,
the kind of blue that checks for monsters in the closet,
the kind of blue that rubs your back until you fall asleep—
the kind of blue that makes you forget
there was even a storm in the first place.

MATT HENRY

OPPONENT PROCESS THEORY

I.

She was screaming terror
of a shadow
dark

like a warbling choir.

All the while,
she makes life
less violent

but is unable to be called upon
this autumn

away

by the shores
of a distant
narrow channel.

II.

Awake
one gets tired of reliving
every empty dilapidated apartment

with cat-piss soaked carpets
and off-white walls.

Asleep,
I'm dreaming
of a scorpion
in the sky

and my heart
is a helium balloon

drifting towards the sun.

MATT HENRY

CANELAB

3

Thoughts think themselves
and get stuck on things like

song lyrics,
movies,
hypochondria;

living in the volatility
between mania and depression.

Which is the delusion:

the intriguing charmer
or brainsick pariah?

2

In the dark
silent chill
of January,

there is tangible longing for
one-million intimate connections:

the ever-lonely married

searching for something
that they already have.

The world
unhinged;

best to show restraint
hidden in the anorex
of the annex.

1

At 30,000ft:

sky shattering sky

mountained clouds monsooning,
blossoming into dark

below 17 silent stars;

thunderous jaws

of wallowing sunset rain
in a red lightning haze.

MICHAEL LEE JOHNSON

WILLOW TREE POEM

Wind dancers
dancing to the
willow wind,
lance-shaped leaves
swaying right to left
all day long.
I'm depressed.
Birds hanging on-
bleaching feathers
out into
the sun.

MICHAEL LEE JOHNSON

CROWS

Tired of hunger
tired of emptiness
late February winter snow—
crow claws locked in
on my condo balcony
steel railings.
Their desperate eyes
focus in on my green eye
sockets—
their search begins,
I go to bed, no ruffled feathers showin—
their imaginary dreams of green—
black wings fly flapping—
the hunt over barren fields—
shadows in the way
late August
summer sun
bright yellow
turning orange
hard corn.

VICTORIA M. JOHNSON

100 WAYS TO COOK CHICKEN DURING A PANDEMIC

Red sauce, white sauce, no sauce
Red wine, white wine, no wine
Cajun, Italian, Mexican, Chinese herbs and seasonings
Mix and match

Pretend you're not lonely
as the chicken talks to you
says you made a delicious dinner
and thanks you for the recipe

Imagine where you'll go
when this is over—
the Genius Bar at Apple
Zumba workout at the Y
Drive to the ocean and jump in
Greet every stranger
you meet at Happy Hour

I long to
Chat with girlfriends in person
even the ones I usually avoid
Attend an art & wine festival
even though I don't buy art,
I just drink the wine

I need my body wrapped in something

other than toilet paper
I need my normal life, not this surreal life
that feels like a Frida Kahlo painting
I need someone to pull the arrow from my heart
and give me a non-sanitized hug

I need to break free of this quarantine novella
and move on to my action-adventure life,
complete with assorted vibrant characters
not on a TV screen or Zoom

But those are fantasies
during a quarantine
For now
converse with the chicken
and surprise it with soup
tomorrow

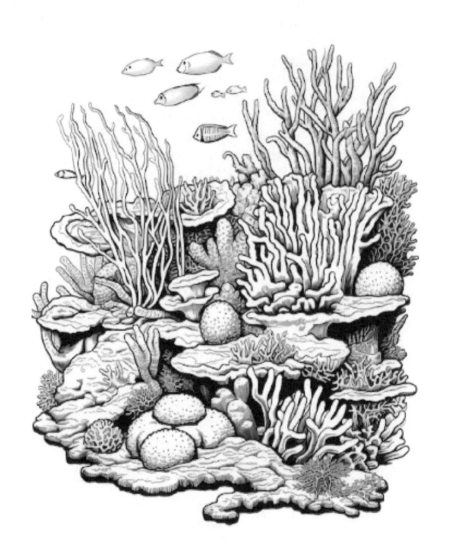

EMILY KERLIN

TWO MONTHS OUT

your death has
taught me to
speak the
tongue of
mourning

passive, softvoiced
verbs, coos like
sobs, the long-
leaning aches of
pause at dusk and
dawn, where I listen

sometimes to the
voicemail you left last
year about slowed
blood, low platelets
and a cancer so small
as to be trivial

and the real culprit,
your surly liver, lame
and scarred from the
bitter, senseless war
waged upon it

still
it's hard to think
of you, not

laughing

harder still to
think of you not
here

doves perch on the
power lines overhead,
and quietly recite the
small sad poems I
have been meaning to
write

EMILY KERLIN

LAUNDRY

when I moved in with your dad
he taught me
to pinch fold
t-shirts,
jelly roll socks,
& square tuck
underwear

since he died
you toss it all
slapdash
in your drawer,
damp, crumpled, balled-up
mismatched

when it's my turn I line up
shirt-sleeves,
smooth out hems, pinch seams,
wrap collars,
square off corners

and deliver them to your room,
since it is not enough that you possess his eyes
and shoulders—you must also
see his hand

DEBORAH KERNER

TURTLE SONG

next morning
life springs into
action a dog barks
in early spring it
swims in canyon
pools along with
turtles
releasing color once
again light refracted
a light mist

drifting off the banks
of a vernal pond
ducks coots black birds

egrets herons
stalking in early
spring frogs sing
the moist earth air

DEBORAH KERNER

UNDER WATERS

if I sit here in the stillness
of slow moves would I be afraid or
would I just let the waters
wash over me cover me and
I would swim them cold
at first but gradually
warmer into kelp forests
golden transparent from the
sun's light stream penetrations   swaying
sparkling world slowed by tidal forces
back and
forth rhythmically
these luminous visions
unknown and unsuspected if
walking two-legged on dry lands

bell-like sounds wavering in
make-believe wet winds until
a melody an undeniably compassionate   melody
electrifies the sea depths as starkly writhing
shadows dance

with intense curiosity rapt
I would watch from these waters the transforming
life forms on the shores my open nostrils flaring
from
the sting of air
my body swaying
to the lullaby of moon tides

HELGA KIDDER

THE WISHBONE

We finally broke it
three months after Thanksgiving,
left you with the short end.

Last year we fattened ourselves,
watched crocus, roses, asters
push through the seasons.

This year we murder crepe myrtles,
cut liriope to the quick,
leave behind I-pad and TV.

Our bones ready to stretch and bend,
to visit foreign languages,
the filigree of turrets, the palaces.

We want to see and live the song,
What a wonderful world,
forget the black and white of politics.

As the hourglass drizzles through
an opening so thin, at first
it seems the sand lies still.

HELGA KIDDER

TIME IS A HUNGRY BIRD

Spanish moss beards the man in the moon
peeking through live oaks.
Tree hair sways in the cooling fall breeze.

A glass of muscadine shines the porch table
and I remember the dance with you
when love was a fragrance between us,
opened us to each other's wishes.
You were smoking a pipe, stuffed it
smoking in your jacket pocket. We giggled,
dazed with wine.

Time flies like a hungry bird feeding,
then disappearing into the forest of days and years.

My glass empty, leaving a tiny trace of sugar.

CRAIG R. KIRCHNER

JOKE'S ON JONAH

Whales communicate, they have a language. They say it has to do with the size of the brain and I'm thinking even a small-minded orca is well stacked. They coo their young, woo during courtship, click for navigation, and sing for enjoyment, perhaps for art's sake. Different pods have different dialects. There is also body language—moves and gestures that show compassion, dominance, and curiosity. There are warnings of predators and obviously discussions of the best places to eat. They probably tell-the-tell at evening gatherings, the stories of the legends—Moby D. and cackles about Ahab's leg.

The opening act on open mic night—a stand-up routine on Jonah being swallowed, carried around three days *in the belly of the beast* and then God said, "Regurgitate this prophet and let the degenerates of Nineveh repent." Clicking and bellows from the audience, and then an Ella-Fitzgerald-like cow singing the greatest hits.

There is probably a poet-per-pod, haiku the most popular form, and maybe chat forums discussing, parenting, politics, blow-hole etiquette. I doubt however, there are racist tropes or grunts for hate. There are whistles and pulses for fear, the most resonant being for sure, the fear of man and his plastic pollution.

CRAIG R. KIRCHNER

ORACLE

The condo faces the woods,
20 feet of grass walkway,
then hundred-year-old trees,
Spanish moss, thick brush,
a stream running through the thickest of it.

There's an indentation, a 'V',
shaped by thick weeds.
Neighbors stop here to admire the trees,
and reflect on their day.
Racoons choose this spot to exit the woods in
nocturnal searches for food and mischief.

I visit often to meditate and ponder,
when all else does not respond or can't possibly know.
There is no trail but an aura.
The weeds flow in the breeze
as the woods maternally absorb the contemplations,
and give back the wisdom of the stream gently,
strategically making its way across the small rocks,
as though there is nothing it doesn't know,
and can't eventually find.

ASHLEY KNOWLTON

FROM A PLANE
HIGH ABOVE CALIFORNIA

the clouds below are vast rolling hills
lined with crops upon crops of
braided cottontails

colliding with billowing silver mountains
jointed with deep furrows and
dark narrow valleys

where weathermen's "atmospheric rivers" must hurry
along
sending streams and streams of so much rain
you can't tell which water belongs to what world

muddling the firmament.

ASHLEY KNOWLTON

HUMPBACK STACKS

craggy sea stacks

sit off the coast

protruding

like bobbing humpback whales

with big knobby heads

ogling the land

H.K.G. LOWERY

PATHOS FOR A BEE

dead
on a sunlit windowsill, I was
petrified of carcass
near coffee,
winged & withering; honey
poured over
porridge, paranoid sugar
might resurrect this spawn of Satan—
but then, there was pathos
for the perished pollinator: I know
there is Rembrandt, Monet
& da Vinci,
but Nature is my favourite artist

BETH MARQUEZ

HOME

It is a twist in the muscles of the chest or the middle of the palm,
   isn't it?
The way so much of the broad, iron sky focuses itself in the body,
like so much heavy smoke collapsing into the smallest black star
into what you know as home. I'm a worrier too. Hitched my chest
to my mother's sighs, shook like my great-grandmother's head

at the September fields clinging to light. It's in the blood.
But so is what is passed across the sheets. So is the sweet burden
of your kitchen table, the rent money, the oven grease, the laughter
in the hallway at the back of the house. Stop for a moment
and rest here, in the dance of summer heat shimmying up the drive,

radio on, porch light calling. Now, tell me what's it like, riding
that feral horse out back. Tell me what its hooves have cost
you. Tell me what you smell in its mane when you get that close.
I have never ridden a horse. Or if I have, I can't remember, not
a thing. Not a thing about how far I was thrown.

JENNIFER MACBAIN-STEPHENS

TEN OF SWORDS

—Inspired by the Dark Wood Tarot

Body on the rocks: ten swords in flesh: what's your handle? We sword ourselves really. Even in sleep we ride hills, climb board game ladders, our invisible horses know the way. Already a couple of souls caught a virus, my compass couldn't catch them, spin them around. I held her love inside of me, the other love, I never knew, but people said he was kind. This murder scene in this fake game tells me she ended the story on her own terms: we enshrine this candy body with raven pecked dreams, brain catalysts, day-to-day breakfasts. A shimmer isn't good enough to describe thoughts, maybe beetles. Tiny hands gesture in the air, tell us to fight or flee, turn on our headlamps in the woods, look for more bodies, that is the point of these swords. We say goodnight to our day of the dead, the car, in a field, the elevator, in bed, a string of yarn: cut. So mortal. So plagued with the past. A new day is always a new day but is it.

A spider traipses up the sword to the body, walks the plank, an opening discovered, wanting to spin, nothing to snip, all to weave.

JENNIFER MACBAIN-STEPHENS

MEET

My son max wanders around the center of the track field. He is a string bean floating through swatches of green and gold. His white shorts, a shark tooth in the grass. He weaves in and out of other boys and girls, his floppy hair in his face. He always seems to be quietly talking, like he is persuading someone to do something, to take on a cause. I spend so much time zeroing in on him, looking for him, losing him in the crowds and sky, finding him, losing him again. I look, look away, find him, lose him, find him, lose him, it's exhausting, this game I keep returning to. Knowing this moment is fleeting, He will never be on this field again, at 6:32 pm, on a May evening, weaving in and out of bodies and ponytails, and cleats. The track meet takes forever and it is over too quickly. Like the sweat on his brow when he runs the mile around the track, it's slow and fast at the same time, is hair flopping, his arms pumping up and down, steady, all the time, in this minute drop of rain, this speck of sand in my palm.

CAROLYN MARTIN

WHALE WATCHING SPOKEN HERE

–Depoe Bay, Oregon

Spring break rain,
migrating pods,
and one uncanny gull.
There! a watcher shouts,
beyond the red buoy,
off the crabber's bow.

I grab binoculars,
confuse white caps
for pluming blows,
wild waves for bluish backs.
Nearsighted eyes cannot conceive
enormity.

But, I can see that bird.
Unperturbed, he doesn't care
the *Samson* needled through
the harbor's eye, escaped
black rocks to chase fluke prints
above the gray whale's dive.

He seems amused
attention's paid to thirty tons—
a tail, a breach, a distant plume
passing twice a yearŽ
his daily stretch of wild coastline,

the shifts of rocky beach.

Regal. Zen. Immoveable.
He can't conceive he's just a gull
and dreams his dovish dreams.
Reincarnates perhaps.
A coastal spirit courier.
A rain-free olive branch.

Five minutes down! the watcher times.
Track south a mile or two.
We ignore the hordes who chase
immensity. We watch wild winds
whip close to shore and fly
into the driving sea.

CAROLYN MARTIN

RESILIENCE

It's the buoyancy, someone said, that keeps
you floating on rejection's sea.
I appreciate the thought, but I'd revise it
to My father's strategy for navigating
waves along the Jersey shore.
When body-surfing tossed/tumbled/crashed
me on the beach– –salt stinging scrapes,
sand sagging my bathing suit– –he schooled me
how to calculate waves' height and speed
and embrace determined choice: with/over/
under/through. His lessons took.
So when editors toss out unfortunately's
or we didn't have the space or we're sure
you'll find another home, dive over/under/
through their words. Then head out to sea
with poems as buoyant as their best.
Float them again and then again.

URSULA MCCABE

TIDAL MOUTH OF THE SHORE

> *"'When you die,' her father told her,*
> *'all the elements of your body wash*
> *into the stream of living things.'"*
> —Kathleen Dean Moore

I am picked up
with webbed paws
by a whiskered otter who
meanders down a stream.

This old body is headed
for the sea.
All the cells, tissues
and organs are molting,
they surrender with no grace.

Algae begins to grow,
there is moss on my face
and so the sea keeps me
at the estuary
and allows my grizzled edges
to scrape the river bank.
Edible plants rock loose
and ride the current-
for anyone else
who awaits death
with their green desires.

Cattail reeds
entangle me up in their roots.

There is still enough of me
to hold my breath
so the marsh wren will
use me for firm footing,
and open its beak.
My goodbye will be a
liquid song
spilling into a misty morning.

URSULA MCCABE

FORTUNATE

an early butterfly came
with white checkered wings

there was no clamor
soft forelegs left a dusty mark
on the daffodil
who is also humble
with its tipped face
and lacey bonnet

sun takes the stage gently
and is the only one here
who doesn't tiptoe around
the new season

we all bow to sun
and know
we are nothing
but mere skin and petals—
lucky to get spring
at all

LAUREN K. NIXON

OVIS

It's in those first months of nuzzling,
soft and babyish, when it settles into your bones;
an elemental journal made of the oxygen, the nitrogen
in the water–your water, your mother's, yours by inheritance.
By the milk you drink. By the soft grass you nibble.
Up it comes through the rock, a holdfast to the earth.

Soon, it will be strontium in your teeth, when you're
not an infant, not a yearling, but in that in-between space
biologically liminal, laying down enamel, echoing the mineral,
gamboling.

Your mother will be gone.
You, down in the meadow, growing fat; up on the hillside, growing
    fleece.
Isotopes weaving into protein tapestries, ready to be made into
    something new.

My pasture is a clean room, where I follow the thread of your thread
in this rich gift of warmth laid into the grave of an ancestor,
and read this record of transit, pause, origin, belonging.
A dance of destinations. I chase phantoms in the mass spec,
sticking pins in the map.

LAUREN K. NIXON

STORM SONNET

A hot, still day. I push through air made thick
with pressure weighing heavy on the land.
I am walking; half-dust, back sweat-slicking,
withering, I follow the dry streambed's strand.
Rain splits the eerie yellow sky, and I
jink downhill, seek haven beneath the trees.
The canopy shifts, distressed, heaves a sigh;
beyond, the storm brings moorland to its knees.
Enclosed, I sink into a soft moss kiss,
tranquil as the stream awakens, swells, stirs.
I am content to wander on like this,
a temporary guest among the ferns.

An hour gone, I emerge into the light;
blinking, I turn my blistered feet towards the night.

SHILO NIZIOLEK

WHEN THE KATYDIDS STOP SINGING

–After Claire Wahmanholm

Mostly, I'll miss the sounds: warblers warbling,
katydids playing the symphony, how wind blowing
through forest sounds like a rushing river or waterfall
nearby, my niece's laughter, the memory of mouths parting.

I can't shrink my desires by pretending they don't exist.

When the world ends, when we choke on the remnants
of the burning wood, the ash thick in our throats like
sarcophagus dust, like mummification, when we scorch
to death under an unrelenting sun, when the waves swallow
us, the ice all gone, starves us, the bees line the asphalt,
drop dead, even you will curl, crust up, your love a mass
extinction, your love an avocado seed, no water left to plant it.

You, who take for granted all that you see before you.

Only I, half-embodied, feel the small feet of the dragonfly on my leg
without brushing it away, holy arbiter of loss denying what is sacred,
watch the katydid draw its strings gracefully against one another,
point to the kingfisher that follows us as we float down the river,
preserve your name, ice-crusted, shell-shocked.

SHILO NIZIOLEK

WHEN ██ KATYDIDS ███ SING██

Mostly, I'll ██████████warble███████,
katydids playing██████████, how wind ██████
██████████sounds like███████████████
█████████████████████████ mouths parting.

██████████my desires ██████████████ exist.

When ████████████████████████████
█████████████████████ our throats███
██████████████████████████scorch
██████ under █████████████ the waves swallow
█████████, starve us, the ████████████
drop dead, ████████curl, ███████your love ████
extinction, your love ████████████████████

You██████████████████████████

████████████████ ██████ ██ ████████████████████
███████████████████████deny██ ████████████
████████████████████against one another,
██████ the kingfisher ████████████the river,
██████ your name ████████████.

SANDRA NOEL

I AM THE WANTING BLUE

I want to whorl my weed in sea pools,
sweep salt-crust from high rocks.

I want to sign my name up the bank,
nosh on clover, leave souvenir shells.

I want to slam up the street,
shock rain-wash with tide silt.

And you, I want you.
I want you to know my rhythm of wave,

my body of waters wants to sea-witch your water.
Let my spice-brine seep slow.

Be water with me. Come home.

SANDRA NOEL

FINNING THE SWEEP OF THE BAY

fish is aware of the shift
    two rocks shoreward
  back as far as the boat
      where waves sculp under-rolls
        weaving a glide-and-pull
         unseen from above

    until in moments of mellow
      a flash of dashing fish shadow

        or if wind blows a ruckus
          the wave chases fish and itself

    but when the rain falls
      the taste of ocean
    is ever so slightly
         different

      but no matter
       for now at least

         fish is still fish
          in this unfathomable sea

JESS L. PARKER

POEM FOR MY UNBORN DAUGHTER

Rocking my son to sleep again one night
I count the many, wooly sheep of things

I might have done throughout the day . . .
I might have boiled a pot of eucalyptus

water. I might have written a poem
for my unborn daughter . . . I might have

climbed the backyard tree and dangled
happily. I might have gazed in the mirror

at the green-eyed woman becoming me.
Instead, I count these many sheep with

wool so knotted, these many sheep with
eyes so grey. I count and sing and shush

my son. I rock the night away.

2

I love how long he has been two
and I want it longer. *Two-and-a-half,*
he corrects me in the Sunday blue
of our backyard, his eyes closed
as the *f* at the end lingers between
two front teeth a little longer

than necessary. He plucks a
fallen maple leaf from overgrown
grass and asks, *what kind of dinosaur
this one's gonna be, mommy?* Then
swiftly answers, *a tyrannosaurus rex.*

This, he whispers furtively, eyeing me
beneath a furrowed brow and too long lashes.
There is poetry in the way he speaks, snapping
words together like an unplanned city

of magna tiles. *How can you tell it's a T-Rex,*
I wonder. He clicks his tongue, buying a beat
and twirls the yellowing leaf between two
fingers on a rigid stem. *Because . . .
she's havin' a very long tail.*

JESS L. PARKER

GAP-TOOTH SMILES

A coral crew sock, limp and open
on the living room rug is a rose
wont to wilt until a toddler plucks it up,
puts his nose in. Now, he is an elephant

trumpeting triumphantly, pudgy little
feet slow-motion stomping. Soon,
he will be an apatosaurus for the sock
is long as her neck—reaches so many leaves
from tippy tops of trees for munch, munch,
munching all around the swamp.

After that, he will be an astronaut but briefly
for his head is bigger than the sock which he thought
might make a helmet and it does for Mr. Popcorns,
the stuffed bunny, whose long, soft ears stand
the sock straight up to Mars.

Someday, unfortunately too soon,
the sock will be a sock again, an annoying flotsam
on the once molten sea of carpet, an unmatched
and redundant garment with a too-thin heel

and wormhole toe. But for now, it is the blade
of a helicopter, whirring overhead as he
gallops the length of our living space,
gap-tooth smiles as wide as this room.

JOEL SAVISHINSKY

EXTREMITIES

No man is an island on *Survivor*. Not only
are there women, but also other competitors
and a crew large enough to fill the jumbo jet
they all must have flown on to get to the set
with their cameras, lights, make-up, editing
console, sound board, toiletries, wardrobes,
caterers, security guards, and enough
concocted angst and PR playbooks to
make hardship look real and yet not
unduly tax the nearby resorts, bars
and clubs sitting just out of frame.

A few coastal bays away, against a backdrop
of towering trees and carefully curated
vegetation, the host of a travel show
records for cable that moments before
she had been the first white woman to
ever witness the sacred initiation rites
of the remote Notlih-Darnoc tribe.
The director calls "cut," and the staff
pack their gear, leaving behind the now-
empty garden of Pago Pago's Grand Hotel.

The morning after these programs aired,
I showed my class a film about the !Kung,
South African hunter-gatherers who, in
their nomadic life, carry all they own across

the Kalahari in animal hide slings the size
of backpacks. Their contents weigh less
than the textbooks of my pre-law students.
The desert community is a network of kin
whose elders tell tales uninterrupted by
commercials. Their pronouncements are
public service announcements. Sitting around
evening fires, each generation adds its stories.
No one is silenced. There is no process of
elimination. In this desert, no man or woman
is an island. The seasons of life do repeat
themselves, but there are no re-runs.

JOEL SAVISHINSKY

THE UN-NAMED

The long dead, long forgotten, with
names that sleep on as well as under

their stones. We cannot even
recall those, four generations ago,

who themselves did not remember.
The names too have been un-named,

their faces erased, though the land
bears the imprint of all they made

and discarded, tried and forsook,
ignored or neglected. The earth's

memory tells us their stories even
on nights when we try not to listen.

Its remains remind us of their failures and
dreams, whose names we have also lost.

It remembers, for our sake,
even those we never knew.

MANDY SCHIFFRIN

THE STARFISH

Life begins in waves;
in the strands of weed,
in the cool of rocks.

Till the star is out
of its depth; stripped and
exposed by the tide;

bereft of haven,
little by little
drying out in the sun.

Pentagrammatic
rage without solace,
living in the air.

But no one evades the
painful crawl back down
to the sea and sky.

Certainly not I.

MANDY SCHIFFRIN

UROPYGIAL

The Mallard sits and preens, chutting
to herself, with one watchful eye on the child;
draws each plume through her bill,
dabs her head back to her tail and
rubs the waxy oil on her chest, meticulous,
fluffing and gleaming her down.

The girl watches the bird, humming softly
to herself, sitting cross-legged in the grass,
chewing on a stray wisp of hair;
the dew is drawn by the material suck,
so that the denim trousers are stuck,
stiff and clammy, to her skin. She shifts.

The duck half stands in wary alarm;
a droplet rolls off her back. She is
watertight; a model in non-stick.

LARRY SCHUG

I'M TOAST

I wake in a large bed covered with thick blankets,
my head on a soft pillow.
I rise from this bed,
dress in clothing I choose,
venture into a house that does not allow cold wind to enter,
a house that has windows that let in light,
give me a view of aspen trees, bee balm turning sunrise red,
chickadees and mourning doves singing,
a house that has a door
that I can lock or unlock at my discretion.
I eat a breakfast, I call it my breakfast
though I share it with a yellow dog.
I eat a wheat field
Slathered with a dairy farm, a maple tree or cherry bushes
without even thinking of apple pickers and farmers with sore backs.
I eat books, write poems on trees, hoping someone will eat them.
I am privileged.
I look in a mirror at my old face haloed with white hair,
Realize I have been privileged a long time.
A thought enters my mind.
You know what that thought is.
You think it, too.

LARRY SCHUG

MOONLIGHT IN A COYOTE'S EYE

When my soul goes the way of all souls,
The journey on which it leaves my body behind,
I would like you to strap the husk of what once was me
To the back of an unbridled burro,
Set it loose to wander a nameless canyon at Ghost Ranch,
Hopefully to be attacked by pack of coyotes,
Though I want the mule to escape, this not yet being its turn.
I desire my body to be torn apart and eaten
In order that I might have a voice
Worthy of howling at the moon with new brothers and sisters.
I want my skeleton to shine awhile beneath a full yellow moon
Rising from behind the silhouette of a dark mesa
Desert mice chewing my bones to dust and wind having its way.
I hope for Georgia O'Keefe, in another go round,
to capture the light in a coyote's eye, a painting with no name.

NOLO SEGUNDO

ON FINDING A DEAD DEER IN MY BACKYARD

I saw them a few weeks ago. My wife called me, something urgent—
so I left the computer and went to see what so excited her.

Three deer, 3 young deer meandering around our ¼ acre backyard.
They look thin, she said—I agreed
(not saying it was not a good sign with winter coming near).

We enjoyed watching them through our plate glass door, their
casual grace, that elegance of walk deer have when unafraid.
They were special, even more than the occasional cardinal
alighting in our yard like a breathing ruby with wings—so
we stayed as still as possible. I told her that deer can only see
what moves, so we held ourselves tight like insensate statues.

Two of these white-tailed beauties grazed daintily on the ground
but the third was drawn to our giant holly tree, resplendent
with its myriad red berries, like necklaces thrown capricious.
I was concerned—something alarming about even deer drawn
like the proverbial moth—safe, I wondered, for deer or tree?

The triplets soon left our yard, as casually as they had come,
and a week went by—then one day a single deer came back.
I say back because she went straight for the holly tree, and
I banged on the plate glass door and yelled as fierce as an
old man can yell to scare off the now unwanted intruder, for
something told me the holly tree would be death to the deer.

She fled, but the next day came back again, again alone, and
again with eyes only for that tree, an Eve that could not say
no to the forbidden fruit—or berries or leaves it appears.
Again I chased her away, and for a few days saw no return.

Then one brisk morning our neighbor called—he saw what
we could not see in the deep green thickness of that holly tree.
The doe lay sleeping under its canopy (so death always seems
with animals, unlike a human corpse where something is gone),
killed it seemed by berries or the leaves of the innocent tree.

I called my township—they said, put the carcass by the street,
we'll send someone to pick it up—but I couldn't, or wouldn't.
Not just because I walk with a cane, and am old and unsure
how such a moving would be done—no, no, it was more—
when I saw the deer lying sheltered beneath the tree it loved,
the tree it died for, it seemed a sacred place, consecrated—
and I could not bring myself to violate nature's holy ground.

Fortunately I have a neighbor who is not sentimental, and he
dragged the dead doe roughly to the curb, and I knew, by
its pungent unearthly smell of death, it was the only answer.

NOLO SEGUNDO

TRANSFIGURATION

It always happens

when I am not expecting

to be immersed —

a subtle wave washes

over me like a

waterfall of air,

the air of eternity . . .

my body then seems

to dissolve, flesh

becomes more spirit

than meat, ego vanishes —

the lightness of freedom,

the lightness of soul . . .

CAROL LYNN STEVENSON GRELLAS

GAMBLE AT A RAMBLE

They ate flowers for breakfast and drank
the sky in the afternoon, they told each

other stories about catching bees
in an hourglass and marking time

with honey, how every day they chased
seeds of dandelions past broken

clouds that hung like billowing sheets
on a clothesline, they said there's a chant

in every word that finds its way to breathe,
and singing is the only means to hear

an honest voice. I watched them play
in the garden, they were like fairies

flying in and out of birdhouses, following
one after the other into an Alice-sized

world. I wanted to ask them what it was
like to live in that kind of wonder, to inhale

magic and blow a thousand breaths
of rainbows through trees, but this was just

a dream, and there was no one
there to answer.

CAROL LYNN STEVENSON GRELLAS

WHEN YELLOW WAS GOLDEN

When you're young, both feet tucked
in your favorite yellow galoshes,

hair braided away from your face,
drops of rainwater glistening on cheeks

ruddy from the wind's playfulness
as it lifts dandelions like butterflies

through the breeze, you don't think about
having a car to get anywhere, your legs

carrying you each morning to school
and back, or the house around the corner

where your best friend Pam lived. The two
of you walking to the Five-n-Dime store

spending your allowance on Cracker Jacks
with toys and baseball cards laced between

candied-coated popcorn, or weekend afternoon
visits to Mr. Peak's dairy, where you'd tow

your little red wagon over the dilapidated old
bridge and bring back iced bottles of fresh milk,

coming home to watch your favorite TV show, two
hangers bent for a makeshift antenna, your parents

sipping highballs in the living room while listening
to Trini Lopez on the phonograph, the needle

catching on a scratch every so often, your mother
giggling as she quickly moves it past its trapped

mark on the 45. You don't realize that one day,
you'll remember this time with such nostalgia

and bittersweet longing, it will seem like a dream
that you try to fall into again and again. And now

that you know what you know about life
and its ephemeral vow, you can't help

but savor those yesterdays even more,
their innocence and fleeting existence,

which might justify your sudden urge to walk
to Target and skip home wearing yellow galoshes.

ANNIE SULLIVAN

SHARK TOOTH HUNTING

Crumbled dirt falls through clamped fingers
As I search for you.
Stones roll away.
Bones are unearthed.
But you are elusive.

Your jagged little points hide
Like unpressed diamonds
Amidst this valley of once ocean-filled expanse

Then, as my fingers sink in
As smooth as shell
You are there

ANNIE SULLIVAN

A SHARK TOOTH SEARCH

Faded fossils crumble as I search for you
Sand shifts
Shins burn
Shells crunch and clatter

Salty water stings my eyes so far down deep
Lungs ache
Starfish stab
Fingers forage and fumble

Silt surrounds me as I scramble through
Crabs scuttle
Hands encircle
Victory is mine alone

MARIANNE TEFFT

CEPHALOPOD LOVE

It is sobering to think
I am much less smart
Than a spotted cephalopod
For I have never learned
To change my color and texture
The way an octopus will do
When he needs to camouflage
Among the perils of his environment
These eight-limbed invertebrates
Know to smooth their dimpled skin
To slide into niches and crevices
And tint their flesh to match the audacity
Of their marine climate
In dire straits they will wrap themselves
Inside an inky veil of obfuscation
They can rewire their brains to brave chilly waters
But I cannot find my way to negotiate
A calculated frigid shoulder
Or read icy signals of a love grown cold

MARIANNE TEFFT

ROSE-COLORED GLASSES

You don't need to see me in my fuchsia parka
To know that pink is the favorite color
Of a displaced Caribbean woman
Or know that I lovingly packed the hot-pink running gear
That carried me countless times across the Causeway
And lifted my wings at the Flying Pig
Beside the raw-silk rose party dress with pleats
Louvered like jalousie blinds
On a day when there is no sun to deflect
I still rock my trusted rose-colored glasses
Not so much that I might see the bright side
But that I might stay in my lane a moment longer
Silence my lips as they cling to a ruby-red glass
And tell me and us that all is peachy
Or surely will be as the silvered day
Beds down in heliotrope dreams for the night

DOUG VAN HOOSER

RUBY-THROATED

You hum as you hover,
  dart like a karate punch,
 retreat, observe, and dive.
You inspect the abutilon bells,
  canna's red mittens, even the heirloom
 pink carnation geranium.

Somehow you wend a way
  into the greenhouse where
 blooms beckon. Glass captures the heat
and you. Blind to windowpanes
  you knock and knock,
 but no door opens to the white oaks and blue sky.

I retrieve a fishing net,
  try to scoop you from the glass,
 the pain of failed escapes.
But I am inept, you elusive
  until you tire, seek to hide
 behind the flowers' batting eyes
and sheepish smiles that enticed you.

I move two pots expecting you
  to sprint, but your wings are spread
 like two hands on the knees, grasping breath.
I take you in hand, a vibrating alarm,
  and bring you out into the summer's hot hug.
 Open my hand, you launch,
a firework that blasts into the sky.
  My anxiety takes flight and disappears
 with you high in an oak's leaf sanctum.

DOUG VAN HOOSER

AUTUMN SCHERZO

Late October, the tree leaves bloom
  rust red, fire orange, daffodil,
 lemon, and varnished oak yellow.
The wind bullies in from the south,
  whitecaps wave on the lake.
 The temperature inflates to eighty.
Is it a gasp or a howl?
  Summer crying don't leave me!
 Or bellowing I won't go!
The squirrels don't care
  as they bound across rippling grass,
 scurry up oaks and hickories.
Change is a heavy rock.
  I can't give up what I know.
 The comfort time has composed,
my private symphony.
  Even the gaps between movements hums.
 For three days the wind attempts
to bring back summer warmth,
  but the sun lays low in the sky,
 won't kindle July heat.
I fiddle with the knob,
  try to bring in a clear signal,
 but it wavers and static cackles.
Wild turkeys cross the road.

PROSE

EDWARD AHERN

THE DOGFISHERMAN

The thigh-deep tide rip pushed his right leg into his left, teetering him. He braced himself with each step, waddling out bandy legged, further and deeper.

Danny pushed into the ebbing tide to stretch his time at the end of the shoal. He knew without looking at shore lights where he was by the bottom- sand, then gravel and stones, then mussel beds, then round rocks covered in weed. Sometimes it helped to try and count the sluggish paces, but he always lost track, diverted by a fish splash, or another fisherman, or his own inward twisting thoughts.

The shoal grabbed toward the Penfield lighthouse but never reached it, knuckling southward into boulders and deeper water where fish sometimes lay. Danny had about four hours to fish before slack low water. He fished the ebb and not the incoming several fishermen had stayed out too long on an incoming tide, been washed off the slimy rocks, and drowned

His favorite hours were between midnight and 4a.m., the dark still when striped bass were active. There was rarely anyone else at the tip of the reef, except, from time to time, for Ralph. Danny worried that he and Ralph were too much alike, given that Ralph was at least eccentric if not a little crazy. Ralph was there that night. And that night he showed Danny something.

"Ralph."

"Danny."

The moon's crescent was emptying out, but there was enough light to see Ralph's face. Concave cheeks sloped into wrinkled lips and missing teeth. Danny thought again that if Ralph wasn't a meth addict he should have been.

"Any luck?" A politely meaningless question, Ralph's rod was bent in an arc indicating a fish of perhaps four or five pounds.

Danny stopped two yards shallower than Ralph, not wanting to interfere with his playing of the fish.

The striper splattered water as Ralph reeled it in. Then, uncharacteristically, Ralph gave the fish slack and it was off.

"Not like you to lose a fish Ralph."

"How long have we seen each other on the reef Danny?"

"Maybe five, six years, now and then"

"You fish like I do. Live like I do too. Ex wife, kids gone. Still no job?"

"Not yet. Surviving on workman's comp. Why the hell else would I be out here at one in the morning trying to catch dinner."

"Yeah. Dunno about you but this time of night, when I can't sleep, it's better for me to be up to my ass in water with nothing to abuse."

"Something like that. Not many people are stupid enough to be out here with us."

Ralph paused. "I think I need to show you something Danny, but you have to keep your mouth shut."

"About what?"

"Easier if I show you. Stick with me."

The instruction wasn't necessary. Ralph had a peculiar way of fishing, but he was usually into stripers or blues and Danny shadowed him. Ralph studied the mottled surface of the water for a minute, then shifted twenty yards to his left and cast.

He hooked up immediately with another small striper and reeled it in. With smooth, unconscious motions he tucked his rod under his right arm, grabbed the fish's mouth with his left hand, and twisted out the lure with his right.

Dropping the lure into the surf, Ralph fisted a knife slung on a lanyard around his neck, slashed the little striper's gills and tossed it back out.

The fish didn't live long enough to bleed to death. Three and four foot blue-black ribbons surged at the fish and tore it apart.

"Jesus, Ralph, what the hell was that?"

"Dogfish, spiny dogfish."

"Did you know they were there?"

"They're out here a lot of nights when I'm alone. I was surprised they hung around when you arrived. When somebody else shows up they disappear. When they stayed I figured they wanted me to show you."

"Holy shit. And you feed them?"

"Yeah. I keep a big fish to eat, but toss out maybe a dozen small fish during one tide swing."

Danny had caught dogfish when he fished with bait at night, and had worried every time he had to reel one in. Over three feet long, snake skinny, with mildly poisonous spines, shark teeth, and black, shiny eyes. Sometimes other sharks in the school would follow their pack mate in, waiting. Even with pliers Danny had never tried to take out the hook, and had just cut the leader.

"How many stripers tonight Ralph?"

"One for me, maybe six or seven for my friends."

"They never bother you, or the fish on the stringer?"

"Never. If I watch close I can see them in the water. There's one old shark that's easier to spot. He swirls so I can see him, then sets up at an angle, like a hand on a clock face. If I wade toward where he's pointing I'm almost always into fish. He gets what I don't keep."

"That's crazy."

"Come stand next to me. Look where I'm pointing. Really look. Look through the surface, into the water, It's dark blue on black, but when he moves you get a glimpse of his belly. There, see it?"

"God damn. That's a shark?"

"See where he's pointing?"

They both brought fish ashore that night. Danny came back to the reef two or three nights that week, but only saw Ralph once. And the fishing while Ralph was there was good. Danny had tried to get Ralph to tell him in advance when he was going to the reef, but Ralph claimed not to know until just before he left his little apartment.

"I just get an urge, a feeling, and I come out to the reef."

Once when the fishing had slowed Danny moved closer to Ralph. "I don't care, but why do you feed the sharks? They just scare away the other fish."

"No, it's the opposite. The sharks are here because the other fish are." Ralph cast and slowly retrieved his swimming lure. "What do you know about dogfish?"

"Nothing, other than I don't like catching them."

"They'd probably be in the top five most successful species—men. rats, cockroaches, then maybe dogfish. There are more dogfish than any other shark, despite that they're heavily fished—their fins get shipped off to the Asians and the rest is processed into pet food and fertilizer. They give birth to live babies, like we do, and their pregnancy is way longer than an elephant's, longer than any other animal with a backbone. They hang out together. A small pack is a hundred sharks, a big one is maybe a thousand. Some live to be fifty. Survivors.

"I, I rely on them—they tell me where to go, where to fish. And I pay them back."

Danny and Ralph sporadically talked as they fished, mostly about the obvious—divorce, lack of money, health problems—but not about everything. Like many men, they hinted at their shortcomings by the absence of information, and over time, in weaving together what had been left unsaid, they sensed the shape of each other's demons, the ones neither wanted to be ashore with after midnight.

They fished together perhaps once a week. Ralph got skinnier and weaker that summer, and Danny, in an unobtrusive way began helping him on and off the reef, started towing Ralph's fish behind him along with his own.

And then Ralph stopped coming. After a week Danny checked with the landlord, who opened up the flat. Nothing. A half a dozen changes of clothes, paperwork from Medicare and Social Security, a few family pictures. Old textbooks on chemistry and a framed diploma—in another life, Ralph had been a chemist.

Nothing else. Danny called the cops, who grudgingly filled out a missing person's report.

Danny fished for another two weeks with poor results, occasionally with other fishermen who knew nothing about Ralph. One night, fishing alone at the knuckle of the shoal, he saw the swirl of a big fish in the shallow water in front of him. Close in, maybe ten yards away. The fish didn't move. Neither did Danny.

The fish seemed motionless but in an eye blink had closed the distance between them to inches. It lay, all of five feet long, at the height of Danny's hips, snout to crotch, but Danny didn't back up. Instead he reached out, avoiding the spines on the dorsal fins, and stroked the fish's flanks, felt its skin rasp his palm. Then, without volition, he put his hand against its snout. The dogfish opened its jaws and gently closed them on the meaty ball of Danny's palm. Danny felt its teeth snick through skin.

The shark, jaws still closed, slowly waved Danny's hand back and forth in the water, churning blood into it. Around them were swirls and splashes as other sharks, many other sharks, swam through the blood cloud.

It's their picture of me, Danny thought, their recognition. After three minutes the splashing subsided and Danny's hand was released. The big dogfish, again without seeming to move, had backed off twenty feet and turned to face away from him.

Danny stood in the water motionless, numbed by what had happened.

The big dogfish swirled again, almost impatiently, and steadied back down, pointing in the same direction as before.

Danny realized that it was pointing toward fish, toward where he should cast. As best he could he mimicked Ralph's actions in moving to the fish point, On his third cast he was into a twenty pound striper.

Danny fished through that tide, ignoring the blood that seeped into the cork handle of his fishing rod. The next night, despite feeling none of the urge that Ralph had described, he was back on the reef. He caught nothing, and saw no sharks.

Three nights later though, he awoke, feeling the pressure of salt water on his legs, almost hearing the broken stone growl of surf. He reached the end of the shoal at 2a.m. at dead low water, a notoriously bad time to fish. But the sharks were there. In the shallow, calm water they flowed like long black hair. His big dogfish was also there, swirling and pointing out to his left.

Danny lost track of the stripers he slashed and threw out into the water, perhaps 25, maybe 30. Around a hundred pounds of fish. Images came to him- a royal executioner, a holocaust prison guard, a priest giving out communion, blood and body all in one. He left satisfied, without a fish of his own.

After August had cooled into September Danny got a call from the Bridgeport police to come to the station and see a Lieutenant Hopkins. About Ralph.

"Have you heard from Ralph Loomis?"

"Nothing. Has something happened?"

"Was he into somebody for money? A bad drug deal?"

"He never said anything like that. Maybe. I dunno."

"You filed the Missing Persons. He must have been a friend."

"Yeah, as much as he had one. The first time I saw his place is when the landlord let me in to check on him. What's happened?"

"We pulled a pair of pants off the breakwater in St. Mary's. His pants. He ever go skinny dipping?"

"I don't think so. He wore his waders like panty hose. I never saw him in the water without them on."

"Was he all right mentally?"

"Crazy? No. Weird for sure. He had cancer pretty bad."

"That's what the VA said. Painful kind. So how come his pants wash up on the breakwater? Not torn, belt in its loops, wallet in the back pocket, money in the wallet. Like he undressed for bed."

"Jesus. Did you find anything else, any remains?"

"Nothing. If you hear something, anything, give me a call."

"Sure."

Danny had the urge again that night and waded out to the waiting pack. Fog was drifting in from mid sound and he would soon lose sight of his sharks. The wind was down, the chop was soft against his waders. He could not quite see where he was fishing into.

As he cast and retrieved, cast and retrieved, he visualized Ralph, dying from cancer, shucking his waders and then his shirt, pants and underwear. He wondered if Ralph had taken off his socks before wading out into the pack, grasping the knife still lanyarded around his neck, and beginning to cut himself, a communion sacrifice to his dogfish.

EDWARD AHERN

TRANSCENDENCE

The deflated body with in and out tubes looked nothing like me. The patchy wisps of white hair on groin and head, the swollen red blotches, the fingers of skin wrapped bone, that wasn't me. But it was.

I was hovering near a soon to be carcass that I could still somewhat feel. And the new me had sight, and heard the voices of those nearby. They were attentive but not kind. Two nurses made side bets on my longevity. Neither went beyond four weeks.

The pain ripping through me for the last year and a half was now a floating presence rather than an agony. The morphine being injected clouded my vessel but didn't hinder my out of body thinking. The membrane between me and my body wasn't porous enough for the dope effects to get through.

I wondered how long my leash was. I—not drifted, not wafted, not flew—shifted to another hospice room and then another, and another. There were often beings like me adjacent to breathing bodies, but they seemed to be in corked spirit flasks, unable to communicate with me or even realize where or what they were. I tried to touch them but we skittered apart, like trying to butt together two horseshoe magnet legs with the same polarity.

Shifting down to the cafeteria, I listened in on staff and visitor conversations. I thought I could smell the coffee and realized how much I missed that ritualized caffeine infusion. On an impulse I—not touched—contacted a staffer and could feel her thoughts, a slurried western omelet of overcooked emotions. I didn't want her life, even briefly, and backed off. She looked vaguely disconcerted.

I felt nimbler than I had in years. I extended to a paper cup of coffee and tried to clasp it. It quivered slightly, the coffee forming expanding and contracting circles on its surface. But the effort temporarily drained me. Getting physical wasn't easy.

A stray thought wandered in. What if we'd gotten things wrong, what if it wasn't the dead who were ghosts, it was the dying, reaching outward from a life they still clung to? Which sprouted another thought. What should I be doing with the month or less that I had left?

Revenge came immediately to mind. First wife? No, that had been equally my fault. Joseph Tissot? The chrome plated asshole had screwed my corporate career. I could find him somehow, pick through his thoughts and use the information to incriminate him. But the thought quickly curdled. He'd go to hell in his own manner and timing, wouldn't need me to accomplish that.

Nice emotional balance for a Newby.

I figuratively spun around. There was a nimbus behind me, a woman I thought.

You're aware of me!

You've been cavorting like a naked drunk in a convent. Scared the crap out of the life supported. I am—was—Helen.

Dan. How long have you been like this?

A week, but we don't look back that much, we're more interested in the time remaining.

We?

It's an ensemble cast, always changing. Once the bedridden you dies, you'll go somewhere else, probably with yourself. No one knows.

As we talked our presences roiled closer together, until we surprisingly were able to touch. It was a high intensity vibration, a pulsating current of old woman that for a few seconds took over my senses.

Wow, that's what a douche feels like.

You're lucky I don't still have periods.

I felt like I needed to sit down, but wasn't sure I was standing. *Helen, can we somehow continue to exist without our bodies?*

Probably not. No one comes back to say hi or tell us where the instructions are kept.

I wanted to smile to show Helen I appreciated her humor, but of course had no face. *I enjoy your candor.*

Maybe not if we were married. My husband left me years ago because I wouldn't coddle his image.

Screw him.

That didn't work, either.

I couldn't smile but could laugh, and did. *Helen, I don't know of a polite way to ask, how much longer do the doctors say you have?*

Two weeks, give or take.

You're good company. Could we hang out together?

You're nice but a little slow, Dan. Why do you think I let you know I'm here?

What about the other presences? Is there some way we can wake them up?

We were hovering in a busy corridor, and staff unheedingly walked through us. I saw a couple of them flinch, so maybe we did have impact.

Some already are, like you and me. But mostly when I try to touch them, they only shudder and skitter away, like there was a bug on their skin. I can't read them.

I noticed the clock above a nurses' station. It was almost three pm, when my wife and son were scheduled to visit. *My family's coming, Helen, and I have to get back to my room. You can come along if you like.*

She hesitated. *Won't you want privacy?*

Nah, they're wonderful people and I'd like to share them with you.

Okay. Advice from something with a whole week's more experience than you have. Don't look into them. Keep your memories as they are.

Her tone was bittersweet, and I knew she'd peeked and been disillusioned. *Okay.*

Sarah and Peter came in a few minutes after we'd shifted into my room. After some initial hand holding, cheek touching and soft loving words, they began to talk across comatose spouse/dad like I wasn't there, asking the staff about treatment, discussing my crappy condition, and planning for when fading got final. Around ten minutes in, Sarah gave a little flinch, then went over and put her arm around Peter. She was silently crying. Fifteen minutes later they left.

I butted back up against Helen. *You looked into her, didn't you?*

Couldn't resist. She's imperfect, but you know about most of that. I may have given her a tiny tweak, just to keep her attentive.

MAGGIE BAYNE

THE RETURN

The late afternoon sun bore through the passenger-side window like a beam through a magnifying glass. These were the perfect conditions for igniting dry trigs, but not conducive to comfortable automobile travel.

"I'm burning up over here," Denise shrieked. "For God's sake, turn up the air."

The long-suffering driver, recognizing that he was defeated, leaned forward, stretching his hand to adjust the temperature inside in the little red car. *Whirrr.* An arctic blast instantly flooded the front seat, providing abrupt relief. The discomforts experienced by desert visitors in July were legendary and late afternoon was an especially unpleasant time of day.

"Are we almost there yet?" Denise prodded. "I want to get out of these sweaty clothes."

Grant, the driver, had experienced a long day, too. His sunburn was itchy, his throat parched and he had spent the entire day squinting beneath prescription sunglasses to navigate the bleak desert highways. On top of everything else, the passenger's continual whining was wearing him down. From Houston to Albuquerque and beyond, Denise's bitching and moaning confirmed for the two of them how miserable this trip had been.

Planning this adventure began during the Thanksgiving holiday several months earlier. Grant and Denise had been sitting by the fireplace reminiscing about how warm the same holiday always was when they lived in Phoenix. Thanksgiving Arizona-style was observed in short sleeves with dinner often followed by a long walk. Phoenix had provided a pleasant lifestyle—exciting, vibrant, hopeful, fresh. But having lived there for so many years, Grant and Denise were not opposed to leaving when career moves dictated.

By the time Grant and Denise moved away, Phoenix was experiencing the inevitable by-products of being a popular Mecca: uncontrolled sprawl, choking traffic, foul air. Like so many other popular destinations, factors that lured newcomers eventually obliterated the fun. Phoenix had become just another city with all of the "usual" problems, far less the exotic oasis and playground it had been in the 1960s.

So, they had left the desert, choosing to experience four seasons and normalcy in the Midwest. Their lives were now relaxed and a good deal more civilized. Autumn in the Midwest was always lovely: a dazzling season accompanied by soft breezes which brought the prospect of another somewhat more ominous season. By the time Thanksgiving arrived, winter was on its way.

It was this deep November chill that spurred pleasant memories of Arizona. Once talk began about seeing the Valley of the Sun, they both grew enthusiastic about that prospect. But commitments had restricted that their return occur during summer months, not the optimum time to enjoy being outdoors or visiting old haunts. July temperatures in Phoenix hovered above 105 degrees. Grant and Denise decided to make the best of summer's heat. Besides, they already had plenty of experience with the desert.

Precautions were taken to ease their journey through the desert during the worst time of the year. Grant had the car serviced, changing belts and hoses, those pesky rubber devices which could snap at the least opportune moments. Like veterans of battle, they recalled the sorts of things that could go wrong while traveling, determined to avoid such pitfalls.

"Really," the passenger began again, "How much longer? Aren't *you* tired, too? Can't we just stop for the day?"

"I want to reach Scottsdale tonight. It's only another hour or so. We have those reservations and can take it easy tomorrow." He needed to focus on something more pleasant, like a good night of rest. Certainly, any attempt to soften the present moment's miseries would not hold up with this audience.

On through the late afternoon's blazing, blinding sun the car sped, its windows shut tight against the unbearable heat, a temporary shelter from the abusive conditions on the outside, mere inches away from certain ruin.

Each year the media retold tales of doomed travelers, who fell victim to a flat tire or broken fan belt in the desert, only to become disoriented and later casualties of the heat. Their bodies would be discovered where they tried to escape to find water or help. Man was allowed to live in the southwestern desert with Nature's permission and on Nature's terms.

Only about another hour, Grant had promised Denise, and kept that thought to spur him on. Even with the comforts provided by the car, Grant was keenly aware of the scorching sun reflected from the hood, sending up visible ripples of heat from the surface, tiny rays bouncing off the red paint. Across the road ahead, frequent mirages of water appeared, giving the impression of a recent cloud-burst. Of course, upon reaching each puddle, there would be no water at all, only a further reminder of the heat's mastery.

Some distance outside of Scottsdale, there began to appear scattered signs of encroaching civilization. The occasional convenience store with adjoining strip mall, sprinkled subdivisions cluttering the horizon with their still raw yards. Buildings dotted the barren soil, like dice tossed with no thought to placement or permanence.

Grant noticed a large gas station/convenience store/snack shop coming into view. "I'm going to top it off," he announced to the passenger. "How about something cold to drink?" His thoughts at announcing such an idea were completely selfish.

"That sounds good," came the response. "Enough of this!"

Grant pulled up to the pumps, filling the tank, then leaned in the driver's window and asked, "What would you like?"

"A big Coke with lots of ice. Thanks."

The store contained racks of chips and munchies, sunglasses and Styrofoam ice chests, all big sellers in the desert. The fountain section was marked off with yellow tape and appeared to be closed.

"Ten gallons at pump 6," Grant declared. "No drinks available?"

"Cans in the verticals," came the reply. "No fountain cause there is no ice."

"No ice? Why not?" Grant asked.

"Because of the water," the young man behind the counter said sarcastically. "Because of the water, man." The cashier appeared exasperated at the stupidity of such a question, sighing deeply while ringing up Grant's gas purchase.

"What do you mean, 'the water'?"

The young cashier looked up lazily, as if he were about to state the obvious. "Because there *isn't* any water, man. Where have you been?"

"Sorry. I don't live around here any more. Is there a problem with the water?"

"Yeah, man," came the reply. "There isn't any. Big story in these parts."

"No water? None? I don't understand."

"Real shortage, man. No rain all year. Started out with rationing and now here we are in July and there isn't any water. Don't you watch the news, man?"

"Guess I missed that story." Grant picked up his change and returned to the car, not eager to share this new information with his passenger.

Denise was peering through the windshield, apparently anticipating a large Coke with ice. When she saw that Grant was empty handed, her disgust was visible.

"Where's my Coke?" she barked. "I was looking forward to my Coke."

"The fountain was closed. And I didn't think you would want a can. The clerk said something about there being a water shortage."

"Water shortage? Where?"

"I don't really know. Guess we'll find out."

They pulled into traffic and headed on toward their destination, eager for the day's trip to end. Grant began to envision their comfortable suite at The Pharaoh, a sumptuous resort constructed shortly before they moved away. The image of that hotel, with its spectacular grounds and lavish amenities, had danced in his head ever since they began to plan the trip. Grant had announced to Denise, "If we are going to visit Phoenix, then we are going to stay at The Pharaoh and do it up right."

Each of the travelers had begun to anticipate how lovely it would be to check into the resort, perhaps take a dip in the pool and linger over a tall, cool beverage. As these most pleasant of thoughts seemed likely to become reality, Grant noticed a dark, gauze-like cloud sitting low on the horizon. At first, he believed this plume indicated a desert brush fire, common on dry terrain, particularly during the summer. He observed that the plume did not rise or spread, but remained stationary. Its color was khaki brown, tingled with green and appeared veil-thin, translucent.

Peering from beneath the sun visor of the car, Grant pointed to his passenger. "Look at that. Is that smoke? What do you think could be the source of that cloud?"

"My dear," Denise said. "You have been gone from here too long. Don't you remember how polluted the air was becoming? It's just junk in the air, car exhaust and dust. We always saw that gunk when we would fly out of Sky Harbor Airport." She looked at the cloak of particles above them, observing its dark color and lifeless motion. "But it seems to have grown worse since we left. I don't recall anything quite so disgusting. To think that people actually *breathe* that stuff!"

"Sometimes the air would look foul," Grant recalled. "But summer rains would usually cleanse the atmosphere, even temporarily. That is quite a sight."

At the corner of Pima Road and McDonald Drive, a large shopping center had sprung up in their absence. "Look, Denise,"

Grant shouted as they approached the corner. "Remember this location? There was nothing here but bare land. I think it was part of the Pima Indian Reservation. Yes, I'm sure this was the spot. Now there is a shopping center."

Denise looked up, less than enthused and noticed the large center with popular anchor stores and bistro eateries. "What is that?" Denise observed. "It looks like a fountain." Clearly what she pointed out was a fountain, a tall granite structure. But no water spilled from the tiers. "Maybe it isn't hooked up yet or something."

As they drove deeper into Scottsdale, Grant noticed an uninterrupted string of cars creeping along the streets. The procession of vehicles moved slowly, winding through the signals as one long multi-jointed creature. "Guess it must be left-over rush hour," he remarked to Denise. "Sure is heavy traffic."

Grant turned into the driveway at The Pharaoh resort and approached the main building. The grounds were lovely, filled with desert landscaping, luxuriously decorated. Now that twilight was approaching, the palm trees were illuminated with colorful floodlights. The main lobby was a tall structure of rust-colored stucco and white columns, resembling a grand hacienda, majestic in the wilting heat.

As Grant and Denise neared the desk to register, they noticed a large placard near the Concierge desk. It read: "Pool closed indefinitely due to water shortage."

Grant retrieved the pen to register and remarked to the desk clerk while he gestured toward the sign, "Say, what's this about the water?"

"Yes, sir. You see, there is a shortage of water throughout the area right now. It has been in the news lately. I'm surprised you haven't heard about it."

"Sure haven't," Grant responded. "But then we aren't from around here. Is it serious?"

"Yes, sir. There is little water to spare. Most swimming pools are closed and residents are asked not to water lawns or wash cars. Here at the hotel, we are asking guests to reduce water use. Our restaurant is closed, just temporarily."

"Really? The Egyptian Room? That is one of the reasons we wanted to stay here. The food is supposed to be wonderful."

"Yes, sir. Five-star rating. But there is not enough water available to keep all our facilities open and the restaurant seemed expendable. Sorry for the inconvenience."

"Is there anything else which will not be available?" interrupted Denise, now growing irritable after her long day in the heat.

"The golf course is closed until further notice. Its upkeep required too much water during the summer. Perhaps by next winter the water supply will be more abundant. I understand that if the water situation continues, electricity will soon become scarce. The power plant west of the Valley apparently uses water to cool its turbines. In a few more weeks, there might be a true electrical shortage." He smiled nervously, to reassure the visitors. "But hopefully, that will not occur."

Grant leaned toward the clerk, as much to prevent Denise from hearing the conversation as to indicate he was getting the inside track of information. "Just what caused this shortage?"

The clerk leaned forward slightly and said, "The water situation began when we received no rain over the last year. We never get a lot of rain. But this year, without any rainfall, the lake levels were down."

Grant recalled that Phoenix received most of its water from a chain of small lakes northeast of the Valley. Through a series of canals, these lakes provided most of the water used by residents.

The clerk continued. "There was minimal water available in a couple of the lakes, but testing revealed the levels to be polluted by a rapidly-increasing bacteria count. So, releases to the Valley ceased and we have been dealing with drought for the past few months. It's difficult, especially when most summer recreation here requires water."

Grant thanked the clerk for his input and the bellman led the weary travelers to their room. The suite, located just off the main lobby, was indeed luxurious, large, and extravagantly decorated. Denise's face brightened when the bellman opened the door.

"Oh, my," she couldn't curb her enthusiasm. "This is lovely. Grant, look at that view."

The view from their south-facing window was impressive, displaying the breadth of the Valley of the Sun in every direction. The Valley appeared bright, clean, sleek, and shiny. The sun reflecting on the stylish high-rise buildings always reminded Denise of a new automobile with recently-applied paint and chrome, gleaming brightly. Phoenix structures were untainted by time as so often was the case in other parts of the country. In Phoenix, few buildings remained to the age of 30. A building of that age would certainly have been replaced with a younger, snappier model.

That khaki blanket was still visible above the shimmering city. Even in the darkness, the mantle hovered tree-top high, a foul substance of uncertain sources.

"Excuse me," Grant addressed the bellman as he was handing Grant the keys, automatically extending his hand in hope of receiving a gratuity. "What is that layer of brown that I keep seeing above the ground? See, there it is by the front palm trees, just above the parking lot."

"Sir, that is smaze, a hybrid of smoke and haze that is always present. I understand that Phoenix used to experience smaze only during winter months when the colder air in the surrounding mountains kept it contained. Now that blanket sits there all the time and frankly, we hardly notice it at all."

"Doesn't it cause problems for some people, breathing problems?" Denise asked.

"Oh, sure," the bellman smiled. "Including me. Some days the weather reports will include health alerts warning against jogging and other strenuous exercise. My doctor tells me that breathing difficulties have increased dramatically in recent years. Many people walk around with special inhalers or wear filters that look like surgical masks. Pretty funny looking," he smiled. "But they seem to help a bit."

These words struck Grant and saddened him. Grant's gratuity-bearing hand was extended to meet that of the bellman and both smiled at the exchange. "Thanks," Grant said flatly.

"Thank *you*, sir," the bellman answered as he headed for the door. "Enjoy your stay."

Grant and Denise were now alone in the room. They both turned to resume absorbing the view from the window. Before them the mountain-ringed expanse spread, here a high-rise, there a palm tree, over there South Mountain.

Winding through a cut in the mountains and trailing among the buildings was a glowing, slinking creature, moving at a snail's pace. Covered with red lights, it crept along like a giant reptile.

"Look at that," Denise said, indicating the red-lighted creature. "What IS it?

"I think it's traffic. Tail lights creeping home. Yes, it looks like an unbroken string of cars headed out."

"But it is such a long line. There must be a lot of cars."

"Yes, well, I think there are a lot of cars in Phoenix now. Traffic was becoming a problem when we left and with the continual influx of newcomers, it certainly can't have improved."

Denise sat down in one of the wingback chairs that faced the magnificent window and the view beyond. "Look at how slowly it is moving!" She paused, reaching down to unfasten her sandals. She sighed and slumped back against the deep rust upholstery, stretching her hands forward to embrace the chair's arms. "I'm certainly glad I am not sitting in a car out there, in this heat." A small smile crept onto her face. It was the first smile that Grant had seen in some time, the first indication that his passenger might begin to relax.

"I know," he said. "Say, let's get something to eat. Since The Egyptian Room is closed, we'll have to find a place to eat. I'll call the Concierge and see if he can recommend a restaurant. Go change if you want."

"Good idea." Denise was glad to change out of her traveling

clothes that had become wrinkled and sweaty.

Grant picked up the telephone and rang the Concierge. Denise could tell from the half of the conversation she heard that Grant was not receiving good news. "Oh, really." and "Is that right?" were repeated a few times. He hung up the phone and turned to share the information.

"Concierge says that there are practically no restaurants open due to the water shortage. Even fast-food places are closed. No water. No ice. No nothing. He suggested that we go to a grocery and buy quick fix items, make sandwiches and have pop from a can. That's what most of the guests are doing."

"You are not serious. We are paying to stay at The Pharaoh and we are supposed to go to the grocery for sandwiches?"

"Actually, he said that several of the grocery stores are closed, too. There is a Safeway store a mile or so from here that is open. It may be busy, so if you don't want to go, I'll bring something back here." Grant knew this scenario wasn't going to play well, so he added, "You can rest and cool off."

"Just use your judgment and get something easy." Denise was tired and dreaded the thought of riding any more today, even for a short distance.

Grant walked through the parking lot to the car. It was about 8:30 now and still not completely dark. He had forgotten how hot the desert can be even after dark, especially in the city proper with pavement and buildings. Grant felt like Hansel stepping into the witch's oven. Deep heat, permeating heat, no sign of breeze. There was a smell, too, in the air. It was the aroma of car exhaust, sweaty people, diesel fumes, suffocating scents of all types. Not the damp of the Midwest at night, the odor of growing corn and fresh flowers. Just hot air mixed with unpleasant auxiliary fragrances.

He pulled out into Camelback Road, to join the continuous slow parade of red tail lights. Traffic was at a crawl, even now long past rush hour. The cars were slithering along, one bumper to the next. Only a few cars made it through each light change and then the traffic came to a complete halt. What had happened? Had there been an accident up ahead? But crossing the few intersections on the way to the Safeway indicated that traffic in all directions was equally slow.

At the next stop light, Grant became aware of the other cars. Each appeared to have only one driver, who sat at his/her post staring blankly ahead, waiting to make the slightest progress. He could not believe the complete lack of horn honking or arm waiving. This was a giant parade of single-occupant vehicles, ridiculous in its appearance, tragic in the result. No wonder the air is so foul, thought Grant as he sat in his car, an air-conditioned capsule protecting him from the environment.

Eventually he reached the Safeway. The parking lot was brilliant with lights and overflowing with cars. The scene reminded him of the shopping frenzy in the Midwest with a predicted snowfall. Scurrying shoppers, heaping their carts, every man for himself. Grant had to decide quickly what items he could take back to the hotel which would be acceptable and somewhat special. Maybe get items for a picnic. He headed for the deli, images of roast chicken and potato salad shuffling before his road-weary eyes. Perhaps a bottle of wine.

As Grant paused ever so slightly to assess his shopping plan, he was hit from behind by an older woman who rammed him with her cart. "Look where you're going, sonny," she hollered at him. "Get out of my way."

Startled, Grant managed, "Sorry." He pulled a U-turn and disappeared down the gourmet aisle, which was nearly deserted. The one remaining deli case held a selection of upscale morsels— chicken and macaroni salad—which sounded delicious about now. Grant and Denise had eaten very little earlier in the day because of the heat and even less saving themselves for The Egyptian Room. Now here he was, in the Safeway grabbing for whatever morsels he could find. Fortunately, he retrieved the last whole roasted chicken in the rotisserie case. It might be fun to sit in their luxury suite and have a picnic of wine and chicken. He was enthused about the spontaneity of such an event.

Grant patiently waited in one of the long check-out lines. People were solemn for the most part, though in every crowd there are some who are never content with the service, the price, something. A couple of check-out lines over, he heard a customer raising his voice to the cashier. The customer was waiving a finger at the clerk, and they both turned their heads generally in Grant's direction. It was a heated but brief conversation, the customer was out the door and the next shopper stepped up.

Grant made his purchases and hurried to the car. The entire process had taken much longer than he expected and now he had to join the red tail light serpent and wind his way back to The Pharaoh. Denise would be starving -- and unhappy. He could hear her taunts already.

Grant was unlocking his car door when the angry customer from inside approached from a nearby car. Grant was startled more by the man's appearing out of nowhere than feeling frightened. He tried to conceal his surprise by saying, "Oh, excuse me. I didn't see you standing there." He smiled then said, "It is really busy in there, isn't it?"

The angry customer stood silent, then noticed Grant's Illinois license plates. "Oh, you from Illinois?" he asked.

Grant relaxed a little, now that he had engaged the man in conversation. "Yes, I am. Used to live here, but it's been a while ago."

"Well, now you come out here and flash your money and think you can just take over," The angry man's voice was rising, as it had inside the store. He walked toward Grant and said directly into Grant's face, "You bought the last roast chicken in there, did you know that?"

"What?" The fact that this man was making an issue out of the chicken more than surprised Grant. "I'm sorry. I didn't mean . . ."

With that, the angry man retrieved a small pistol from his grocery bag. The parking lot lights reflected on the barrel only momentarily before the man shoved the gun against Grant's stomach. Just as quickly, he pulled the trigger, returned slowly to his car and calmly drove away. Nothing more was to be done, his task apparently complete.

The flash of pain was intense. Grant remained on his feet, stooping over slightly, his hand grasping the point of entry. His shirt was already wet from the oozing wound and Grant knew he was seriously injured. He stood there, not knowing what to do. The angry man was gone.

In the middle of this brightly lit parking lot, amidst the madness swirling around him, there was no one to ask. No one to help. Grant knew he could not maneuver well enough to find a telephone. Even if he did, should he call an ambulance? Call the police? Standing there with his life source dripping from his newly-received injury, Grant knew that he had one course of action. It was to get back into his little car and rejoin the slithering trek of cars and return to The Pharaoh. Perhaps he could drive right up to the doorman and get some help. Besides, Denise was there and she was the only person for 2000 miles who cared anything about him.

Grant managed to adjust himself in the seat so that he was comfortable. The pain of the wound seemed to have lessened somewhat, or at least he ceased noticing quite so much. The red flood was a tidal wave now, soaking his shirt, his pants and dripping onto the floor mats. Through his mind flashed concern about how hard it would be to clean up, dreading how upset Denise would be.

Driving carefully now to avoid any sudden movements, Grant pulled the little car into the never-ending stream of vehicles moving past the Safeway. Once they joined the procession, each driver became a part of the whole, like a segment on a centipede, headed along with the rest of the creature to some unknown destination.

MAGGIE BAYNE

THE WALK

Tom climbed out of bed and gently opened the balcony drapes. The room was instantly flooded with bright sunshine.

Despite efforts to be quiet, Susan stirred, rubbing her sleepy eyes. "What time is it?"

"Sorry. I didn't mean to wake you." He glanced at his watch. "It's 6:15."

"Oh, no. I thought we were on vacation. You promised we could sleep a little later."

"Just look at this glorious day." Tom turned to face his wife, raising his arm toward the broad balcony view.

In the distance, the early morning sun reflected off the Gulf waters. The sky was clear, colored an alluring shade of turquoise. Soft, fluffy clouds were scattered across the horizon.

Susan sat up, tugging at her long blonde hair. She glanced at her husband, a tall, youthful man of 50, who remained trim and fit. He wore the beginning of a deep tan. "You look great standing there with that smile. Vacation seems to agree with you."

"We don't see a view like this at home, at least not very often." He returned to sit on the bed next to her. "I can't sleep when there is a day like this waiting."

Susan crawled across the bed to Tom and leaned against his leg. "OK. You win. You finally agreed to take a few days away from work." She patted his knee. "I have to give you credit for that. So, we'll do whatever you want to do today."

Tom leaned forward on his knees, eyes focused on the horizon that spread before them. "You have to admit this is remarkable."

"I can't recall ever seeing such a beautiful sunrise. Towns along the beach sometimes have fog, haze or some obstacle to ruin the morning. Maybe approaching rain clouds or extreme heat. That last trip to Phoenix was brutal. Even this early in the morning, it was already way too hot to do much."

"Let's go out right now and walk down to the beach." Tom was on his feet, moving around the room. He pulled on a pair of chinos hanging nearby. "How long will it take you to be ready?"

"A quick shower and some make up . . ."

"No, no. We're on vacation. We can take a stroll on the beach, Susan! For heaven's sake. Let's go."

Susan quickly dressed in shorts, tee, and flip flops. She gathered her blonde hair into a ponytail and donned a Cubs baseball cap.

Tom nodded. "That's more like it. Besides, you already look beautiful."

"What are we waiting for, Mr. Barrett?" Susan trotted over the door.

Tom grabbed the camera, the room key, and sunglasses. They traipsed to the elevator and rode down in near silence. They strolled through the hotel lobby and out into the early morning air.

"Smell that ocean." Tom stopped a few feet from the parking lot, arms spread wide, head back. He inhaled deeply.

Susan copied his stance. "You are right. That air is wonderful. I guess we are really in Paradise."

"Actually, it's called Florida. Clearwater, I believe. Last one to reach the sand buys breakfast." Tom sped toward the sand a few yards ahead.

The two tourists ran to the surf, Susan flopping on to the sand.

"Looks like you're treating us to breakfast." Tom stood over her victoriously, hands on his hips. "Right now, you look about 17 all relaxed and wearing shorts."

Susan sat up and opened her eyes. "Guess I should relax more often. It seems to agree with both of us."

Tom shaded his eyes with his hand and scanned the beach front. "I see a nice little café over there. We could eat out near the beach.

Sound good?"

"Absolutely." Susan got to her feet, dusting off excess sand. "Only this time, no sprinting."

Tom took her hand. "But we have to walk barefoot and stay in the sand."

Susan inhaled deeply. "I used to hate the smell of the ocean. It always reminded me of dead fish and salty plants. Now I appreciate how unadorned it is."

"I've always liked the beach. It reminds me of when I was a kid playing in a sand box. Our neighbors had a sand box. I loved to run my fingers through the sun-warmed sand and dig in my toes."

Susan said quietly, "Maybe we should think about retirement in Florida or somewhere in the south with moderate weather."

"I thought you liked the Midwest area."

"I do. I love Chicago and all it has to offer. Plenty of opportunity and sophisticated dining, museums, shopping. But the pace is draining. You recognize that, too. It might be a nice change of pace, something we both would enjoy."

Tom laughed softly. "Retirement is a long way off. But you might be right about a move."

"We can both think about it." They approached the hostess at the café.

"Two for breakfast?"

"Yes."

They were seated beneath a large blue umbrella at a glass-topped table. As they savored their omelets and fresh juice, they spoke little.

Tom signaled the waitress for more coffee, then turned to Susan. "Were you serious about leaving Chicago? I mean, we've never really talked about moving."

Susan shrugged. "Ever since we've been married, life has been a whirlwind. Your career, my job and the boys. That's going to change one of these days. Eric will be going to school next year and Andy the year after that. The nest will officially be empty. If we are ever going to take time for ourselves, that would be the time to do it."

"It sounds like fun, doesn't it?"

"We could dress and act like this every day. No more snow plowing or parkas. No Florida state income tax, either."

"That's right. Say these eggs are great, aren't they?"

"Yummy." Susan swigged coffee. "So, what are we going to do today?"

"Let's go back to the hotel and change. Then we could take a nice long walk through town, see some shops. Pick up some souvenirs for the boys. Later, why don't we plan a nice evening out —do the town."

"Sounds perfect."

They returned to the hotel, sandals in hand, to get dressed for a day of leisure.

"Do you want to take a cab?" Tom asked as they entered the elevator for the afternoon's outing.

"No way. Walking is too much fun and everything is so close by."

They stopped at a little boutique near the hotel and bought T-shirts for the boys. Tom saw Susan admiring a bracelet in a glass case. "Why don't you try it on?"

"I don't need another bracelet." She shook her head. "It's just rather interesting."

"What are all those little silver discs?"

"Those are names of Florida beaches. See?" She turned on tiny disc to reveal the name Daytona Beach.

"Let me get that for you."

"Don't be silly. It's really cute, but I don't need it. Thanks anyway."

They walked several blocks in all directions around the hotel. When they returned, Tom stopped at the concierge's desk and discussed dinner plans.

"Dinner at 7:00. Plenty of time to take a swim," Tom announced as they entered their room.

"You know, I've had plenty of sun for one day. I'm thinking about a little nap before dinner."

Tom said nothing. "If you don't mind, I think I'll go ahead and take a swim. Is that OK?"

"Normally, a swim would be very tempting. But I'm parched. I can get freshened up, soak in the tub before dinner.

"Suit yourself." Tom changed and stuffed a towel into his backpack. "I'll take the key in case you are in the tub when I get back." He dropped the key into the pack.

There was plenty of time for a swim. But Tom's main objective was to return to the boutique and buy the bracelet for Susan.

As he headed away from the hotel, Tom felt confident about his plan. He knew Susan would like the bracelet. It was the type of spontaneous purchase that he had always enjoyed. The bracelet would also confirm what they had discussed earlier. They were both excited about the prospect of someday moving to Florida. It was an option that seemed to make sense from the moment they both expressed their attraction to such a move.

Tom returned to the boutique and greeted the saleslady. "I was in earlier with my wife and she was admiring a silver bracelet with little discs."

"The discs with the beach names." She nodded. "I remember you. She really liked it, didn't she?" The sales lady walked toward the case. She opened the top and removed the bracelet, its discs making a sweet, tinny noise as it dangled in the air.

"That's it, all right. I'll take it."

The clerk placed the bracelet in a box. "Would you like it gift wrapped?"

"Good idea. Thanks."

Tom put the package in his backpack. "Thanks for your help."

"She will enjoy wearing that bracelet. We sell a lot of those. It seems like women like to show off the bracelet and relive their trips. You'll be surprised how often she will wear it."

Tom headed back toward the hotel, cutting through a small park to reach the crosswalk. On the other side of the street, the pool was waiting, blue and inviting, surrounded by swimmers and sunbathers. Beyond the pool, the ocean beckoned, large and luxurious compared to the confines of the pool. He changed his course and headed to the wide-open spaces of the beach.

At the crosswalk, the mid-morning traffic was heavy. A light pole marked the pedestrian crosswalk. On its pole was a large sign and button: "Push the button to cross the route." Tom pushed the button several times and waited. His eyes remained focused on the beach and he could almost feel the waves and sand beneath his feet. He turned his eyes toward the oncoming traffic. The parade of vehicles was broken intermittently, the flow controlled by traffic signals scattered along the route. *These are people in a hurry*, he thought to himself. *There is so much to see here. Perhaps they are missing Florida's beauty.*

Watching the approaching vehicles in the next block, Tom saw a break in the traffic. He watched carefully as it neared and decided to cross.

Even though the light had not changed, Tom stepped forward, eyes glued on the traffic. He could feel his thigh muscles tense as he prepared to sprint over the lanes to the lane divider.

Here it was. His chance to go. Tom shouldered his backpack, grasping one strap with his hand to assure it wouldn't slip off. He leapt into the roadway and began walking briskly. He could feel his adrenaline kick in, as though he were meeting with a new client for the first time.

Around the corner a white SUV got the turn arrow and bolted into the roadway at the same time as Tom. The driver had been delayed when the turn lane arrow disappeared and he had been anxious to continue. The arrow snapped to green and he scurried off.

Tom was focused on the gap in the continuous string of cars and did not see the white SUV swing in from the side. He heard nothing to announce its arrival until the moment it hit him.

Whoosh.

Tom was aware that he was being tossed into the air. For a brief moment, he was reminded of riding in a playground swing at Jeffers Elementary School. Up, high above the ground he was propelled. Then he realized he was falling quickly. That was the last sensation he experienced.

The driver of the car felt the impact on his right front bumper. The jolt of the collision stunned him.

"What the heck was that?" Jeff, the driver, asked his wife. He turned his head immediately looking for another vehicle. "Was that a car? Did it drive on?"

The entire episode occurred very quickly, seconds perhaps.

His wife Dorothy, swung her head around in all directions. "No, I . . . I don't think so. I don't think it was a car."

The windshield of their car showed the effect of an impact. The pattern in the glass resembled a spider's web and covered about half of the width. A deep-set center to the web appeared to show where the greatest impact had occurred. Circles of damage radiated out from the center like ripples on a pond.

Jeff pulled over immediately and stopped the vehicle. He still could not identify the object which he hit.

Dorothy was focused on finding out what happened. But she could feel the sense of panic rising up in her throat. She looked immediately to the right side of the vehicle and saw something lying on the ground.

"Oh, Jeff. There is a shoe lying over here. It's large. Probably a man's shoe." She raised her hand to point.

They both hopped out of the vehicle for a closer look. A man was lying face down just to the right of the vehicle. He was bleeding profusely from the head.

"Oh, my god." Jeff stood over the man, hand to his mouth. He could barely breathe.

Dorothy began to hyperventilate. Other vehicles began to stop.

A man from another vehicle shouted, "I've called the police. They are on the way."

No one else spoke. The man on the ground remained motionless.

In seconds, a siren was heard. Two policemen stopped and

immediately went into action. One officer began diverting traffic from the lane. The other man called for an ambulance and began talking to the onlookers. What had they seen? Which direction was the man walking? Was he alone?

The officer approached the man and reached over to check his pulse. "He's dead." Once the ambulance arrived, the officers checked the victim for any identification.

Despite all that had happened, Jeff was struck by the mechanical precision with which the proceedings were conducted. The officers and emergency personnel must have been through countless similar experiences, resulting in an orderly routine, long-rehearsed and synchronized.

The officer who had been directing traffic opened the victim's back pack and removed several items, examining them carefully. One was a small slim gift-wrapped box bearing the name Edgewater, a boutique a short walk away. The officers discussed the matter and the first officer on the scene took the back pack and headed toward the shopping area.

The second officer identified himself as Officer Taylor and spoke to some of the assembled people. Once he had taken some information from the members of the crowd, the bystanders drifted off.

Officer Taylor walked up to Jeff. "Have to check with these folks first. They will likely leave the scene. Shouldn't take long and I will be right back with you folks." He smiled weakly to Dorothy. "You OK, ma'am?"

"I think so." She remained seated on the curb, head drooped forward.

Jeff joined her on the curb. "Are you OK? The EMTs are already here. Perhaps they can help."

"No, I feel a little foolish. They have other people with real issues to worry about now."

The two remained seated on the curb while Officer Taylor completed his interviews with spectators. He returned to Jeff and Dorothy and squatted down to be on their level. "Sorry, that seemed to take longer than expected. I'll bet you two are burning up out here on the pavement."

"Where is the other officer?" Jeff asked, shading his eyes to look around.

"That's Officer Oakley. He went to track down an item in the backpack to see if there is any indication about the victim."

Jeff shuddered. "Victim. It sounds so awful. What if you can't figure out who it is. I mean, what about his relatives?"

"We have ways of finding out. Sometimes when there is a lone pedestrian, no car or anything, we can find some clue which leads to more information. It might take a while but we can usually trace the identity."

Jeff shook his head. "You know, I feel so awful about all this. I swear I didn't see him. I was just turning and the light was green. There was a noise but I didn't know I had hit anyone."

Officer Taylor made a note in his file. "The victim was walking against the pedestrian light. It appears that he was taking a dangerous chance and he lost. We have had a number of fatalities on this very road in the past weeks." He continued jotting. "I need to see your license again, please. I see that you folks live in the area."

Dorothy replied quietly, "Yes. A few miles away."

"Well, other officers will be here in a few minutes. They will photograph your car and the street, look for detailed information. We will need to take a full statement from you both. Since you live here, we can do that within 48 hours if you would rather go home and relax a bit first."

Jeff looked at his wife. "Yes, I think we would prefer that. Just tell us where to go."

Officer Taylor handed a card to Jeff. "Here is a little map and phone number if you have difficulty finding the building. Just come in when you feel up to it." He quickly returned to the squad car and drove off.

The rest of the officers had arrived and were photographing the vehicle and the accident area. Jeff asked one of the photographers if they could remove their vehicle. A few more shots were taken of the passenger side fender and windshield and Jeff and Dorothy drove off.

*

Officer Oakley entered the Edgewater store and was greeted by the saleslady.

"Do you remember selling a bracelet this afternoon? The gentleman was wearing shorts and carrying a red backpack. Here is the package and sales slip."

She examined the paper and parcel. "Why, yes. A lovely man. He bought it as a gift for his wife because when they were in earlier today, she had admired it so."

"So, his wife was here with him?"

"Yes. They were from Chicago, I think. Staying somewhere nearby because he was on foot. Is something wrong?"

"I don't know yet. His bag was found and I was just checking to see where he might be staying."

"Well, I'm sure he will appreciate getting back the bracelet. He was very excited about giving it to his wife."

"Thank you, ma'am. You have been very helpful."

Officer Taylor had found a hotel key in the back pack for the Outrigger Hotel. An Illinois driver's license from the victim's wallet showed his name to be Thomas Anderson.

Before he encountered the victim's wife, Officer Taylor contacted Officer Oakley on the car radio. He confirmed that the victim's body was at the morgue and that both officers were available to interview the victim's wife. He waited in the parking lot of the hotel for Officer Oakley to arrive then got out of the car when he saw the other squad car pull in.

"So, everything lined up?"

"Yes, I think we have the name. A saleslady from a boutique sold a bracelet to a man this afternoon with a red backpack. He was from Chicago and his wife was staying with him here. Looks like a match all around."

"Let's go. This is never easy so we might as well let her know and get the ID done."

They stopped at the desk and asked for Mrs. Anderson.

"Their room is 1810. I hope nothing is wrong. It's not every day that police officers come to our hotel." The desk clerk strained to smile.

"We just need to talk to her. Thanks."

The officers walked to the elevators and pushed the Up button. Neither officer spoke during the trip to the 18th floor.

TRICIA CASEY

A SHARK TALE

For as long as I can recall, sharks have been thrilling to me. I saw Jaws as a kid but, oddly enough, it was the next-door neighbor's pool I was afraid to swim in, perhaps the most controlled swimming environment we know. Never the ocean where we are surrounded by beauty and peril, seen and unseen.

I grew up three blocks from one of the most beautiful beaches in the world—Kailua Beach on Oahu. The only shark I ever saw growing up was a baby hammerhead that washed up on the beach at Kualoa Beach Park one summer while at Girl Scout camp. We'd just come in from paddling an outrigger canoe into deeper waters. I was ten and instead of being gripped with fear, I looked out at the water and wondered where its mother was. I know more now. Nearby Kaneohe Bay is one of the world's largest breeding grounds for hammerhead sharks. In May and June, female hammerheads give birth to 20 to 40 live pups each and then leave the area, and their pups to fend for themselves. It was one of those pups we saw that summer. There are, quite literally, thousands upon thousands of Hammerhead pups in the bay at that time. Which can attract larger sharks.

During my Junior year of high school, a woman by the name of Marti Morrell was snorkeling with a visiting friend just about 100 yards from her beachfront home near Lahaina on the island of Maui when she was attacked by a 15-foot Tiger shark. The water was only six or seven feet deep and they were just outside of the reef which can offer some protection from larger fish. Her friend was only brushed by the shark as it swam by and she swam toward shore screaming for help. Nearby swimmers paddled out to try and assist but multiple Tiger sharks had joined in on the attack. It was too dangerous and, sadly, too late.

Every story of an encounter with a shark is dramatic, even when it isn't. These creatures are, for most, the stuff of nightmares. The ocean is unforgiving to those of us who live on land. We are already at a disadvantage the moment we enter the waters where we ultimately have little or no control over what happens. Add to that, the visceral fear of drowning or, worse, being eaten alive, and we have a foundation for drama. Marti Morrell never stood a chance. It wasn't a test bite where she could be helped to shore with what would certainly have been life-threatening injuries. The sharks took both her legs, an arm, and more.

What came afterwards is what kept my attention. The responses from the public, the tourism industry, government officials, scientists, and native Hawaiians were a cacophony of passionate disagreements. For some time, the State of Hawaii conducted a shark eradication program about every ten years to take large predators found within Hawaiian waters, trying to control fears and the risk to swimmers and, by extension, the tourism industry. At the time of Marti Morrell's death, it had been 13 years since the last eradication program. State officials were increasingly aware of sharks' importance to the ocean's ecosystem, not to mention the input of scientists who insisted that these hunts were ineffective. Additionally, sharks have a cultural significance to native Hawaiians.

'Aumakua are the ancestral spirits of parents (makua) and their children (keiki). 'Aumakua are believed to inhabit either animate or inanimate objects including living creatures. For many families, their 'aumakua inhabits a shark. To arbitrarily hunt sharks is to risk killing an 'aumakua's physical form. While some sharks were taken in the months after Marti's tragic death, the program was dramatically scaled back and, eventually, eliminated as researchers proved the futility of eradication but, more importantly, as shark attack victims came forward and advocated for protecting the creatures.

This series of events was transformational for me. I absorbed everything I could get my hands on related to sharks. This was the very early days of the internet so it was newspaper articles, books, and searching microfiche at the library. *Shark Week* on Discovery became a holiday of sorts for me. I watched shows over and over again and began to know facts and theories about sharks that made me look pretty good on Jeopardy from time to time. And as access to information opened up to us, I searched for more and soaked it up. But why? I was certainly fascinated by the topic but I also marveled at the hubris of humanity in trying to control the uncontrollable, a creature in its natural environment where we are the ones out of place.

In 2004, we moved to New Hampshire, an hour away from the ocean and the furthest I've ever been from it. The ocean here is so cold but I try to dip my toes in at least a couple of times each summer. It's not just the cold that keeps me in the shallows, though. Ten years ago, Great White sharks reemerged in the waters off of Cape Cod thanks to the blooming numbers of protected gray seals. The sharks' return led to the founding of the Atlantic White Shark Conservancy (AWSC) and the debut of Cape Cod on Discovery's *Shark Week*. There have been a few physical encounters between sharks and humans, including one where a young boogie-boarder died as a result of his leg injury.

I am unabashedly fascinated by the ongoing research and exciting findings by scientists both professional and citizen. For nearly ten years, I've been aching to go on a cage dive to see sharks. I had an opportunity to do so seven or eight years ago but I chickened out. In the meantime, I kept watching the shows, reading the articles, and digging online for more. I started following the work of AWSC online and through social media. And I kept thinking about that cage.

On a sunny day in May 2021, in the midst of the COVID pandemic, I acknowledged that my marriage had been quietly falling apart for years but I hadn't been in a place to deal with it. Doing the math, I knew that in about four years, my youngest would be preparing to graduate from high school and we would be on the verge of becoming empty nesters. And I would be on the verge of turning 50. The pandemic, working from home, and the quiet that enforced lockdowns and social distancing provided, left some space in my busy mind to ponder what had become of the *me* I had been so long ago. My passions felt muted, my many interests largely set aside, friendships untended, and personal health and well-being long-neglected. Both of my natural parents had died in recent years and my younger sister was lost to us due to severe mental health diagnoses. I was lonely and felt like I'd lost control of my life's direction.

That day I started "50 before 50," my bucket list of goals, experiences, and learning that I wanted to accomplish by my 50th birthday in August 2025. There are small, silly things on it that wouldn't seem to warrant a spot on a big list like this, but they were all part of getting back to me. Here are some of those items:

Read 50 Books.
In four years. No problem right? But I hadn't read an average of a book a month in years, something my mom would be shocked by if she were still here. I was always a voracious reader, until I wasn't.

Get a Brazilian Wax.
You laugh but I was always curious but too scared of the pain. And then I recalled the ectopic pregnancy that almost killed me 20 years ago. Or the appendicitis three years ago. The physical pain of losing my mom and then my father. So I did it. And now I do it every month.

Get a Tattoo.
Again, I was afraid of the pain and could never decide what I wanted on my body forever. I got my FIRST tattoo last summer in England along with my then 15-year-old daughter and it's a discreet little shark. And I love it.

Learn Gaelic.

That is one tough language but it's beautiful and I've taken a few semesters. I'll keep at it. It's part of my heritage.

Lose 100 Pounds.

It's not about a specific goal weight but about being healthy, happy with my body, and physically capable of taking on the adventures on my bucket list. I'm 55 pounds down and counting and I have started to love myself in a way I haven't in a long, long time—if ever.

Start Up Yoga Again.

I started yoga 17 years ago. I stopped about 12 years ago as my career took off and my kids became more active, choosing the pressures of a busy life over my own health and wellbeing. And make no mistake, it was detrimental. I remember how good yoga made me feel. So in September 2022, I started up again at the same YMCA I've always gone to. And I am absolutely stronger and more flexible. My recovery from other physical activities such as running, which I don't enjoy until I finish, is better. And the peace and quiet in my mind when I practice twice a week is a welcome respite from a noisy world and a noisy life.

Get SCUBA Certified.

I went SCUBA diving once in college in Hawaii with a certified dive master. It was amazing. I got seasick floating on the surface when we went up to change our tanks and it cut the dive short for me. For years, I avoided boats and anything on the ocean other than swimming. Seasickness is awful. But there are some pretty great ways to combat it so I start my lessons in September 2023.

Go On a Shark Adventure.

I've done three now and the fourth one is later this month for my birthday. I went out with a AWSC scientist in October 2021 on a small boat, guided by a spotter pilot and we located a dozen Great White sharks in waters off of Cape Cod just 10 - 15 feet deep. Not one of those sharks was tagged so I helped record them on a GoPro for identification. Recently, the AWCS scientists released a population study announcing that approximately 800 individual Great White sharks have visited the area in the last four years. I went on a free dive in June 2023 off the North Shore of Hawaii with 10 other passengers. I was the second one in the water and immediately observed dozens of Galapagos and Sand Bar sharks swimming about 20 feet below our boat. Later a Scalloped Hammerhead and a small Black Tip shark made an appearance too. It was, hands down, the most amazing thing I have ever done and not for one moment did I experience fear or anxiety, even when a six-foot Galapagos swam up to within about eight feet of me, looked me in the eyes and swam away.. Later this month, my son and I are going on a cage dive off of Cape Cod.

Adopt a Shark.

In August 2022, through a charitable contribution, the first shark tagged by Dr. Greg Skomal that summer was named White Shark Tricia. She was an 11-foot beauty whose tag was placed that month. The following winter, four months of satellite data was downloaded, showing where WS Tricia had been. I won't see the twelve months of 2023 data until winter 2024 but in July 2023, this goddess came back to Cape Cod from wherever she wintered, passing four times with the requisite 50 yards of one of the buoys placed around the Cape between May and December of each year. Anyone with AWSC's Sharktivity App can find her there now. The buoys are pulled up at the end of "White Shark season" because the Nor'easters here make it impossible to leave them safely there.

Dive Tiger Beach in the Bahamas.

About an hour west of Grand Bahamian Island is an area in the ocean where a sand bar brings the depth to just about 20 feet with astonishing clarity. And it is there where divers can interact with Tiger sharks, as well as several other species, up close and personal. Tiger sharks are among the top three most deadly in the world. They are beautiful, complex creatures and they are where my fascination with sharks began, 30 years ago, with the unfortunate demise of Marti Morrell. You must be SCUBA certified for this experience, hence my earlier goal. This is the pinnacle of my "50 before 50" list. To interact, in immediate proximity, with my favorite shark.

Get Published.

Over the years, I have been encouraged so many times to consider writing. My accounts of parenthood and other ridiculous moments in life, as well as the ability to tell a story that draws in a crowd, is what fosters this encouragement by friends and family alike who would forward my accounts to strangers for their enjoyment, coming back pleading for more. I stopped writing about 16 years ago, soon after my second child was born. This is, in my mind, the scariest item on my bucket list. And here is where I reveal a secret I've never told anyone: I have always wanted to be a writer. I chose practical professional pursuits and did not give in to the luxury of developing my writing into something more polished and built for consumption. What if I'm no good at it? What if I don't have the discipline to master it? What if no one likes it?

The last two years have given me a fresh perspective on my approach to life and how I live it. I have always claimed to be open-minded. But I was passively open-minded where I needed to be actively so, pursuing and exploring, open to opportunity and absurdity. And I needed to allow myself the freedom to absolutely fail trying, again and again. I have learned to be more forgiving of myself and others. I have been practicing giving up the control I so fiercely wrangled throughout my life and letting life happen freely and spontaneously. And I am embracing the things that call to me and thrill me, even if they are scary.

For me, it all started with sharks.

TRICIA CASEY

THE GIFT

During the summer of 2015, my mom was diagnosed with stage four non-small cell adenocarcinoma. Lung cancer. She'd been a smoker for over forty years and her very talented oncologist at Dana-Farber in Boston had been able to tie the "accelerator" on her cancer to a specific gene and to her smoking. She'd had this cough for a long time that she repeatedly blamed on post nasal drip. But a year or so before the diagnosis, the cough changed. It evolved into paroxysms of coughing. Paroxysm. I have loved that word since I learned it. Until I didn't. Until I witnessed it from my mom.

Mom and I had a complicated relationship. Most mothers and daughters do at some level. Ours involved stories that don't belong here but they do belong somewhere. Suffice it to say, our complicated and often difficult relationship became very simple in a moment and with an easy decision on my part. In a moment, I let go of the hurts and the grudges and erased the boundaries and walls I'd carefully erected over the years to protect myself and my children. In a moment, I chose peace with my mom and to be a part of whatever came next in every way that I could.

She and my dad lived in mid-coast Maine, about three and a half hours north of me in New Hampshire. She opted to fight the cancer with a treatment regimen of radiation and chemotherapy at Dana-Farber so she spent weeks at a time with us. I flexed my hours at work to be with her whenever I could, especially during consultations and her initial treatment and when they biopsied the tumor that had wrapped itself so wickedly around the bronchioles of her lungs.

During the first meeting with the oncologist, Dr. Barbie, Mom was so overwhelmed that, at one point, she stepped out of the room telling us to continue without her. I had been taking all the notes in mom's notebook so we could refer to it later. It was then, with Dad, that I asked Dr. Barbie the question. "How long?" He paused, knowing exactly what I was asking, and said, "Conservatively, maybe 15 months".

On the drive back to New Hampshire, Mom suddenly said "Damn! I forgot to ask him how long I have." There was silence in the car. Dad and I knew. I'd written it in the notebook that my mom would read through later. I knew I had to tell her, that she couldn't come across that in the book on her own. I took a deep breath and said "I asked." She looked at me, startled. "You did?" I nodded slowly, glancing at her as I drove north on I-93 through rush hour traffic leaving the city. "Well?" she said, "how long do I have?". "Fifteen," I whispered. After a moment she laughed and said "Days?" somewhat incredulously. "Months?" she said, this time more subdued and I nodded. And then she cried. Hard.

A lot happened in the weeks and months that followed. Mom's treatment was tremendously and unexpectedly successful. In February 2016, Dr. Barbie nearly bounced into the room for an update and reported that not only had they slowed the cancer that had spread throughout Mom's thoracic region, the primary tumor had shrunk and showed no signs of growth in months. Dr. Barbie spoke of a study he was doing that mom likely qualified for and which was showing real promise. Mom and Dad went home to Maine to continue her treatments from there while we waited to hear more from Dr. Barbie.

In April, something strange happened. It mimicked an episode Mom had in November where she was disoriented, in and out of lucidity. Dad checked her into their county hospital once again. She was taken in for a test where they were going to look at her heart and the technician said he remembered doing her test in the Fall. Dad was surprised and didn't know about the test. It turned out, the results of the test were never reported to my parents in the Fall and Mom hadn't been lucid at the time so didn't recall it. What they learned in November, but never reported and didn't treat for, was that Mom was in heart failure and had just 65% functionality of her heart. By April, functionality had shrunk to 35% and there was nothing left to do.

At the beginning of May 2016, Mom entered Hospice Care at home. Her sisters and step-brother came to visit. I brought my children up for Mothers' Day weekend. I came back a few days later. Saturday, May 15 was the beginning of the longest days. One of Mom's sisters and her husband were with me and Dad. Mom hadn't been conscious that day. Late in the evening, a little after midnight on the 16th, Mom became incredibly restless. She tried sitting up but could not. My uncle propped her up from behind while my aunt, dad and I held her hands and tried to calm her and talk to her. Mom called out to her parents. She kept saying something to us over and over again that, at first, I couldn't understand. It was almost like "I-O-U". Her words were so slurred. Whether it was the morphine or her state, I don't know. But suddenly I understood. She was looking right at Dad and I, somehow urgently, saying it over and over again. I said "We love you too, Mama. We love you too." My dad said it, my aunt said it. And then she relaxed some.

The Hospice nurse was so kind when we called. I worried, you see, because Mom was so restless and we'd already given her the maximum dose allowed on the bottle of morphine to keep Mom comfortable. The nurse said to go ahead and give her more. I worried "what if I give her too much?" Quietly and kindly, she said "It's okay." And I realized, of course, that was the point.

Mom settled down after we gave her more morphine and slept peacefully through the night.

It we then, around two o'clock in morning, after she had called to her parents, after she told us once more that she loved us, that I wrote this poem:

The Time Between

This is the time between
An occurrence seldom seen
When ghosts of those before
Gather near for to implore
Walk away with us now
To the after . . . show her how
Release your hold on those you love
Drift and watch them from above
Peace now at the scene
This is the time between.

At about 7:30 on the morning of Sunday, May 15, just one week after Mothers' Day, Mom took her last breath while I held her hand.

It is an incredible, terrible gift to be with someone when they die. My mom and I were the only two people in the room when I entered this world who were also in the room at the moment she left it. This strange realization occurred to me in those moments and I held on tight to that as I wept and whispered goodbye to my mother who, despite our complicated and often fractured relationship, I loved deeply and with every fiber of my being.

I dreamt of her that night and we talked. I have dreamt of her many times since then. I welcome the inevitable pain of the sadness of missing her because it is accompanied by the warmth of her visits in my dreams. And I will always cherish the hardest moments in my life, holding my Mama's hand to the end, for the gift that it was.

KEITH HOERNER

SWIMMING THROUGH SHADOWLANDS

Deep below the lake's murky surface, there sits—intact—a house. A two-story structure of Carpenter Gothic details like elaborate wooden trim bloated to bursting. Its front yard: purple loosestrife. Its inhabitants: alligator gar, bull trout, and pupfish. All glide past languidly—out of window sashes and back inside door frames. It is serene, and it is foreboding. Curtains of algae float gossamer to and fro. Pictures rest clustered atop credenzas. A chandelier is lit, intermittently, by freshwater electric eels. And near a Victrola, white to the bone, a man and a woman waltz in a floating embrace.

KEITH HOERNER

SWIMMING BACK TO SHORE—WITH NO SIGN OF YOUR FOOTSTEPS IN THE SAND OR SIGHT OF YOU ON THE HORIZON

I.

Foam sloshes 'round my scuffed black leather wingtips, laps up the ankles of my rumpled dress slacks, turns khaki to the colour of murky brown. Onlookers furrow their brows, incredulous I do not see I am in danger of drowning, that if I don't make a move for it, the water will continue to rise until it covers my soon-to-be-bald head. What they do not realise is I have already failed at drowning—and floated a near corpse ashore. Can they not see my sopping clothes; the now sea-weed green tweed jacket; my wrinkled, white translucent skin? Their water is returning to the sea. I have survived my Biblical Flood. I am coming up for air, not suffocating. My exploded lungs have been cauterised; I now breathe shallower: but calm and sure.

II.

I look for you, but waves wash you to another shore, an island uncharted, perhaps, to inhibit me from finding you. Did you suffer so? Rather than buoy you up, did my selfishness climb squarely on your shoulders and thrust you downward? Push you under into the electric bosom of a bloom of pulsing jellyfish... until it was you who passed away? Or did your shocking beauty simply meld with theirs, escaping me as I first wondered? My hope is you did get away. My prayer is that you are dry and safe and contented. Even if it means

I cannot be with you.

III.

I may not be dry, but I am drying out. I have always had a dry sense of humour, a British sense of humour, I like to think. Admittedly, I can be droll. My odd obsession with court jesters remains a curious thing. Was it their tomfoolery or their role in history? I don't know. Whatever it might be, you used to laugh at me more than the TV. I cannot hear you laughing now. So it begs the question: when did you turn it off? When was it you stopped laughing? Or was it me —in one of my sardonic rants—who thought he had had the last laugh?

IV.

You were always a giver. The problem is I'm a taker, was a taker . . . for what it's worth. And givers and takers are a mismatch. I did what takers do; I took all you had to give, emptied all your pockets and filled them with rocks: one for each of my character defects. So you stretched out your arms and tried to swim away, but sank. Yet upon the first swirling rush that separated my grip on you, you dropped my rocks and swam untraceable among the camouflage of coral reefs. So, here I am.

V.

Yes, I stand. I'm not buckled at the knees as before or dead as expected. The lifeline you threw me caught 'round my neck, but it worked. It was the one time when looking in the end of a bottle, I actually saw a ship, and with it the possibility of steerage to a new land . . . dry land. Its pasted, miniature masts and cotton-twill sails still able to bear my living freight and move me to a healthy destination. You equipped me to survive the flood in the face of self-harm. How can I repay you? By letting you go? By not even thinking to follow you.

VI.

The small ship, pulled out for embarkation, is now crushed to bits beneath my feet. Peer close, and I might even pass for the Giant Polybotes, bane of the God Poseidon, standing on a shipwreck from the battle of Nisyros. A broken bow floats out to the Aegean Sea. An anchor pulls the splintered spine of this ark into the pit of a dark swell. I was supposed to find Terra Firma by Noah's mandate as one of a pair. I beg you. But I'll force myself to understand, if I am to go at it alone.

VII.

If it is what you need, I will unabashedly say it aloud, "I no longer drown myself in bottles anymore, thanks to you." So I will stay clear of the companion way and wish your sails full billows to get you to your place of secret solace. I will not follow you. But I will always think of you. And if you will allow, I will tightly scroll this missive and slip it into this bottle here, then toss it far in the direction I hope will one day reach you.

BETH MATHISON

SWIMMING WITH THE SHADOW

She floated on her stomach, lazily kicking her legs to stay afloat. She'd always had trouble with swimming fins, finding them awkward and unnatural. Instead, she preferred to wear simple water shoes, and stayed close to the water's surface, breathing through her snorkel and mask.

The water in the Mexican lagoon was clear, showing the sandy bottom and the dark tangle of rock on its edges. A few bright fish swam in front of the rock, rays of sunlight hitting the white sand and swaying ocean kelp.

Salt and fresh water from the nearby cenote mixed in the shallow pools of the lagoon, and the water was not always clear. The surrounding land protected it from rough waves and wind.

Today the water was clear, and she named some of the fish swimming with her. Parrotfish. Tang. Sergeant Major. Chub.

It was good to know names.

To know the way they lived, how they interacted with their surroundings. Life was simpler here–stepping down a craggy rock stairway to slip into the warm water. Another world, shedding the life behind her.

The fish largely ignored her, and she gave them space. She floated on, spreading her fingers in the warm water.

A shadow appeared near the bottom of the lagoon, black across the bright swath of sand. A form, moving its head and tail sleek and dark.

There was no reason to be afraid.

She had seen other sharks, although never in the shallow pools. She wondered briefly what brought it here–food, environment, danger. In deeper waters she had seen the nurse sharks, whale shark and the reef shark. She didn't recognize the shape below her, but it was small, and guessing by its size, a juvenile.

Kicking to stay afloat, she watched the shadow move across the sandy bottom, heading toward the deeper ocean waters. Her questions of why it was here unanswered.

In a moment it was gone.

She was left with the fish, clear water, and the sun warming her back.

BETH MATHISON

SPRING HAIKU

New tree buds drooping

From a blanket of white snow

Spring, it laughs again

NANCY MACHLIS RECHTMAN

KEEP, DONATE, THROW AWAY

Sarah crawled into the closet and found the box with the bright yellow shopping bag peeking out of it, crammed into the far corner. She pulled it out. The contents were covered in tissue paper which she carefully removed, and there was the quilt. Sarah stared at it for a minute, and then carefully took it out of the bag. It was exquisite, made up of 5"x5" squares of gold and blue and white and mint filled with delicate flowers and baby animals. Her eyes filled with tears. When the package from her Aunt Daisy had arrived, Sarah had found it too difficult to take the quilt out, unwilling to deal with all that it represented.

Her hands began to shake. Her beloved aunt had made the beautiful quilt, hoping that one day, in spite of everything, there would be a sweet baby to be comforted by it. Her aunt had passed away shortly after finishing the quilt, so she had never learned the truth. About how lives fall apart, even when everything is done with the best of intentions.

After all, Sarah and Myles had entered into their marriage with eyes wide open. Or so she had thought. After living through the bitter divorce between her parents when she was in high school, Sarah had taken her time when it came to finding a life partner. And once she met Myles, she was amazed at how he checked off all of the boxes in what she was looking for in a man. She never expected to find anyone who was as in sync with her as Myles was. They had met one day when she was trying to balance two pizzas and five soft drinks (in a drink holder, but still . . .) as she got on the elevator in the high-rise where she worked. A man in a hurry was so busy yelling into his cell phone as he charged off the elevator that he nearly knocked her over. Just as the drinks were about to crash onto the floor, a man behind her suddenly leapt forward like Superman and grabbed the drink holder with one hand and steadied her with the other. Sarah had mumbled a thank you to him as she tried not to succumb to the hypnotic intensity of his gaze. It turned out that he worked for the architecture firm one floor above the ad agency where she worked. His name was Myles and he insisted on escorting Sarah to her office to make sure she was in no further danger of being knocked over on the way. She felt compelled to explain that the food was for several of her coworkers who were celebrating the first day of spring. Myles thought that was a charming idea and asked her to go out to dinner with him that night so he could celebrate spring with her, too.

One date turned into many dates and their love deepened with each new season. It turned out they both loved the same historical fiction novels. And they were both big action-adventure movie fans, always going to the theater the first weekend of new releases so they could form their own opinions before the reviews came out. And most enticing to Sarah was when she discovered Myles was a picnic guy. He loved bringing gourmet sandwiches and salads and a bottle of wine on their hikes and finding a place by the water where they could just sit and eat and talk. Or lie down on a blanket and make love in secluded spaces away from the rest of the world, listening to the music of the birds and the water bubbling past them. Their conversations went on for hours, always finding something to discuss. Even the silences were easy. The following spring, he proposed.

"Are you sure?" Sarah's mother had fretted upon hearing the news.

"Mom!" Sarah had said. "Can't you be happy for me?"

"Oh, honey, it's not that I don't like Myles. I like him very much," her mother insisted, even though she had never actually met him. "It's just that love never seems to last. And I don't want you to get hurt. We get sold a bill of goods that there's always a happily ever after like in the fairy tales. But life is tough, and the reality is, there is no happily ever after. You're just lucky if you can tolerate each other after the sex goes stale."

Sarah's mother didn't have any filters. After so many years of dealing with a mother who never had an unspoken thought, Sarah was no longer taken aback by her mother's bizarre utterances. But she didn't want to be pummeled by that constant stream of negativity again. She knew the downside of marriage. She had watched her parents tear each other apart. She knew what she was getting into. She told this to herself repeatedly. She did know what she was getting into, she was sure of it.

And maybe if they had been dealt a different hand, things wouldn't have fallen apart. If her damn body had worked like it was supposed to, like everyone else she knew, maybe their lives could have been perfect. Or at least better. Having a baby was a natural act, wasn't it? You have sex, no birth control, and at some point, the pregnancy test has a plus sign. And nine months later, there's your little bundle of joy. But instead, test after test had a minus sign, month after month, year after year. The hormones she was on made her moods swing so erratically, knocking her completely off balance until she was sure she would never find her way back to equilibrium again.

"I love you," Myles would say after every trip to the fertility doctor. And he would repeat "I love you," after every single negative pregnancy test.

"How can you possibly love me?" Sarah would cry. "I'm broken and defective. I'm a pitiful excuse for a woman."

Myles would hold her as she sobbed, murmuring that she was all he wanted. That it was fine with him if they never had a baby. "We can have a great life with just the two of us," he once assured her. "We wouldn't be tied down. We could travel, we could go out whenever we want, it could just be us. Would that be so terrible?"

Sarah had looked at him, dumbfounded as his words reverberated through her head. Never have a baby? What was he saying? But she was too afraid to ask, to find out it had all only been her dream. But later that night when they were lying in bed and she was staring at the ceiling as Miles snored softly, she began to wonder. Was this why he never blamed her, never fell apart? That having a baby wasn't really what he had ever wanted at all? She thought back to the sweet moment in time after they got engaged and before they were married. When everything seemed possible and the love they had could conquer any possible roadblocks in their way. She remembered talking with Myles about having children. She was sure they had been on the same page as they sat on a park bench, her hand in his.

"Do you definitely want to have kids?" Sarah had asked, searching the depths of his eyes.

"Of course I want a family," Myles had assured her.

"How many kids?" Sarah had murmured, nuzzling his neck.

Myles had chuckled. "Let's start with one and see how it goes," he had teased. "Or we might change our minds and get a dog. Dogs are pretty easy."

Sarah remembered she had been startled, but had decided he was joking. "Or a cat," she had smiled. 'Cats are even easier."

They had both laughed. But now she wondered what he had been trying to say. And if his real meaning had flown right over her head.

As time passed and there was no baby and she felt herself getting more depressed, more desperate, she saw something new in Myles's eyes. The eyes that had once been full of fun and adoration had become veiled. She saw the momentary flash of avoidance when she'd mention that she was ovulating, and it would be a good time to try again. After all the disappointment and heartache, she felt all hope slowly wither away until she was an empty shell.

And she not only pulled away from Myles, but it had become too hard for her to be with her friends anymore. Her happy, fertile friends. The friends who had still tried to include her and Myles in their gatherings. But they were the only childless couple in their group, and it was like getting stabbed in the gut every time they were surrounded by adorable babies and rambunctious toddlers calling for Mommy or Daddy. The final break had happened at lunch one day with her closest friend, Katie. Katie and her husband Zach had also been trying to get pregnant for almost the same number of years as Sarah and Myles. Sarah and Katie had become even closer with their shared pain. Sarah knew that Katie was the only one of her friends who could truly understand what she was going through.

"I hate the way everyone always looks at me like I'm the most pitiful woman on the planet," Sarah had said as she bit into her bagel and lox with extra cream cheese at their favorite deli. "Damaged goods."

Katie looked uncomfortable as she took a small bite of her salad. "I know," she said.

"It's like they don't know what to do with themselves," Sarah continued. "Like they feel sorry for me but they don't want to look like they're pitying me so they say things like maybe we should adopt or maybe we should stop trying and a baby will magically appear . . ."

Katie nodded as she put a tomato in her mouth.

"I know you understand, and I thank goodness every day that I have you to talk about this with," Sarah said. "I couldn't imagine trying to get through this all alone. I mean, not really alone since it's me and Myles trying to get through this together, but we're not really together since he could have a child with anyone he wanted, you know? He doesn't really get it, either."

Katie started crying.

"Katie, what is it? What's wrong?" Sarah asked.

Katie shook her head.

"Tell me!" Sarah insisted, a sickening lump forming in her stomach.

"I don't know how," Katie began. Then she started crying again.

"Just say it," Sarah whispered, as she realized that she already knew.

"I'm pregnant, Sarah," Katie said softly. "I'm sorry."

Sarah felt the shock rattle her body. But she couldn't ruin this for Katie. This should be happy news. Wonderful news. "Katie, that's amazing! That's fantastic! I'm so happy for you!"

And she was. But she also knew she was losing her best friend that day. And the gender-reveal party the following month just amplified how alone she was and how awkward it was to be around the people who used to be her friends now. Everyone cheered when the center of the cupcakes was revealed to be pink, including Sarah. But inside she wanted to die.

And after that, Sarah found ways to say no to any invitation, and told Myles to go hiking with his friends on the weekends and that no, his overnight camping trips didn't bother her. And she stayed home, not answering the phone, not making plans, just curled up on the couch with their two rescue cats, Artemis and Tiger Lily for company. And eventually, friends stopped calling, even Katie who continued to try to keep Sarah in her life. But it hurt too much and Sarah wasn't up for the charade of being fine anymore. And at some point, Myles and Sarah stopped talking about anything that mattered. Sarah retreated further and further into herself until one day, Myles didn't come home. He texted her to tell her he needed a break and was staying with a friend for a while, but he couldn't do "this" anymore. She knew what "this" meant, and she didn't even blame him. Except for telling her by text.

"Coward!" she had shouted, flinging the phone across the room. Artemis and Tiger Lily had jumped, but then settled right back down next to her on the couch. Sarah started to sob. "Why would he want to stay with me?" she cried. "He never really wanted kids in the first place, did he?" And Sarah suddenly gasped. Was that true? Did Myles ever really want kids or had she ignored the blaring red flags along the way? Had she been so sure that their love could conquer any problem, even when he tried to tell her? "This whole marriage was about me and the baby I wanted," she whispered. "I ruined everything." Artemis and Tiger Lily gingerly climbed on top of her and settled onto her stomach. She stroked the cats as they purred, with tears streaming silently down her face. "I became my mother," she said dully. "I swore I wouldn't, but I did. And I pushed Myles away just like she pushed my dad away."

Now, one year later, Sarah was going through the detritus of her life as she prepared to move out of what had once been *their* apartment–alone. Myles had filed for divorce shortly after that fateful day when he told her he couldn't do "it" anymore. At least the divorce hadn't been nasty like her parents' divorce. After all, there was nothing to argue about and no children to fight over, so everything was very civilized. And Sarah's mother could practically be heard biting her tongue every time they spoke, trying not to say, "I told you so," even though Sarah could hear those words coming through the ether, unspoken, yet clear as a bell.

And as she now tried to decide what she was keeping, what she was throwing out, and what she was donating, studying the three boxes that she had labeled for each option, there was the quilt, bringing back all those longings and feelings and anguish in a flood that engulfed her as she sank into the floor. Tiger Lily and Artemis were trying to fit into the same empty box that Sarah had labeled "Keep," and she watched them play. Thank goodness for her sweet babies–without them, she would have dissolved into nothingness. They were what had tethered her to the world during this past year of solitude.

Sarah turned around and started pulling more bags out from the bottom of the closet. She found luxurious sheets and towels she had forgotten about. And then several cut-glass bowls and teak serving trays with handles that were wedding presents that had never been used. There were two blenders that they had never bothered to return in unopened boxes. She put all of these into the large cardboard box labeled "Donate."

And then she stopped. Once she finished, what was next for her? This was not a future she had foreseen. Divorced, alone, her life barreling like a train that had jumped the tracks towards her 40s. No real friends anymore, a job that no longer brought her any joy, a mother who made her crazy, and an absent father who now lived in California with his new family and who texted her every Sunday after his weekly golf game to say hello and ease his guilt about abandoning her.

Sarah curled up on the floor with her head in her hands. Artemis and Tiger Lily rubbed against her legs, trying to cheer her up. Their loud purrs were motorboats, and Sarah stroked their silky fur as she thought of floating away out on the ocean. Then she looked down at the quilt. She knew she couldn't go on like this. It was untenable to constantly be so alone and so miserable.

She tried to remember who she had been before meeting Myles. She had been happy, hadn't she? Content? And she had had friends then. And fun. Her favorite thing had been to dance. When she was young, she had begged her parents for dance lessons and finally, they had given in as long as she kept up her with her homework and brought home straight A's. And once she was older, she loved going out with friends to clubs and dancing the night away. She'd have a few glasses of white wine, shake off her self-imposed shackles, and feel freer than she ever felt at any other time in her life. Her body would move to the beat, and she'd close her eyes as men would come up to her and start dancing in rhythm with her. She'd move with them, sensing their desire for her, until the next guy would come along and she'd find herself with him, dancing to his beat, feeling beautiful and desirable. And so the nights would go. Eventually her friends would pull her away, her dance partners pleading with her to stay for one more dance, but she'd promise she'd see them next time, and she and her friends would leave, exhausted and exhilarated. She had sworn no more one-night stands after several disastrous encounters with different men, so she had made her friends promise to never let her do that again. And they had all promised to watch out for each other and leave together whenever they went out.

Sarah missed those days. When her body wasn't the enemy. She and Myles would dance occasionally if they were at events such as weddings, and they'd have fun when they did. But they didn't go to clubs on a weekly basis. Or really ever. Clubs had been reserved for her single days and it became more and more clear that in so many ways she was saying good-bye to the person she had been before she and Myles married. But wasn't that what happened to everyone at some point?

Sarah had blamed Myles for the divorce, for not understanding the pain she was feeling, for shutting down. But she was finally taking responsibility as well. And she realized that maybe things weren't so one-sided after all.

Just then, her phone buzzed. She looked at the Caller ID and saw that it was her mother. She sighed and then answered it.

"Hi, Mom," she said, trying to sound cheery.

"Hi, dear," her mom said. "I just wanted to see how the packing is going."

Sarah surveyed the mess all over the floor. "It's going fine, Mom."

"When do you have to be out of your apartment?"

"At the end of next month, Mom," she repeated for what seemed to be the millionth time.

"Do you have a place to live yet?" her mother asked, an edge to her voice.

"Not yet," Sarah admitted. "I'm not even sure where I want to live." She paused. "Geographically, I mean."

"What are you talking about, Sarah?" her mother said sharply. "You have to be out of your apartment in less than two months, you gave notice at your job, and you're thinking of moving to another city just like that?"

Sarah counted to ten silently. "I don't know what I want, Mom, I just don't know. Maybe it's time for me to start over completely. I've been thinking about California maybe," she said, bracing herself.

"California!" her mother practically shrieked. "Did your father talk you into this? Now it all is starting to make sense. He'd do anything to hurt me, including taking you away from me!"

"Mom, Dad didn't talk me into anything. It's something I've been thinking about for a long time, getting a new start. I haven't even talked to him about it yet. And how would he be taking me away from you when you live in Florida and I'm in New York?"

"We're still on the same coast, Sarah," her mother sniffed, as if the answer was obvious. "If you move to California you'll be on the other coast, across the country, on *his* coast."

Sarah smacked her head in frustration. "Mom, do you realize how ridiculous you sound?" she asked. "No one owns a coast. I only see you a few times a year as it is. If I move to California, nothing will change."

"Except you'll see *him* all the time," her mother muttered.

"Doubtful," Sarah said. "But even if I did, that doesn't mean I'm on anyone's side, Mom, please. I don't even know if I'm going to move there. But I'd like to get a fresh start, and that's a pretty good place to do that. I'm stuck, Mom. I can't seem to move on. Not just from Myles, but from everything. It's like I'm standing in quicksand. I need to go somewhere else, where no one knows me, where I can drop all the things holding me back and get away from the person I've become. I want to be happy again." She suddenly realized she was crying. "Mom, I need you to understand, this is nothing against you, I need to find someplace, something to in my life to help me change. Can you please try to understand this?"

She heard her mother sigh, but then there was silence. Sarah sniffled and tried to stop crying.

"And you haven't said a word to your father about any of this?" her mother finally asked.

"Only that I'm moving out of the apartment next month," Sarah told her.

"Well, you need to let him know what you're thinking of doing," her mother said icily.

"I'm not really sure what I want to do," Sarah said, trying to remain calm. "But I know something needs to change."

"Moving won't change who you are," her mom said firmly.

"True," Sarah said. "I just need time to figure things out."

"And moving certainly won't bring you any closer to having a baby," her mother declared.

Sarah inhaled sharply. "Mom! I'm divorced. I'm about to be on my own without a job. I'm getting closer to 40 now. The odds don't seem to be stacking up in my favor at this point for adding a child to the mix."

"You need to find another man," her mother insisted.

"Mom, I'm not looking for a man so that I can find a baby daddy!" Sarah practically shouted. "I mean, if I really want a baby, I can do it on my own. I can adopt and raise a baby on my own." Sarah suddenly stopped talking. Why hadn't she ever considered that option before? If she still wanted a baby–and she did–why not adopt? And why not consider raising a baby on her own? Plenty of women did it.

"Well, good luck with everything," her mother said brusquely.

"I'll talk to you later this week and you'll let me know what you've decided. Unless you decide to keep me out of the loop."

"Mom, I promise you that won't happen. I love you," Sarah said. But her mother had already hung up.

She put the phone down and picked up the quilt, staring at the three boxes in front of her. "Keep." "Donate." "Throw Away." Where did the quilt belong? She suddenly realized where it belonged. And the idea of adoption started swimming around in her head. Could she do it? Should she do it?

She thought about the love she and Myles had once shared. It had felt so real. Had it been? Was everything in life just temporary like a cloud that disappears after you look at it too long? Or could feelings be permanent like the smooth granite boulders they used to climb at the state park?

Sarah hugged the quilt to her chest and rocked back and forth. Finally, she picked up her phone again and scrolled through her list of contacts. She took a deep breath and tapped a number. She held her breath for a moment, until she heard his voice. "Myles? It's me." Her heart pounded, but she plunged ahead. "Do you think we can talk? Like in person? There's so much that needs to be said, don't you think?" She listened. "Because I feel like we never had the conversations we should have had. And we didn't really try to work things out after a while, we just let it all dissolve. Maybe we should have fought harder for us. And I'm not blaming you – or me. It's just what happened. But maybe it didn't need to happen that way, you know?" She listened for a moment. "Yes, dinner tomorrow is great, thank you. See you then." She put the phone down and realized she was shaking. She didn't know what would happen when they finally got together, but she knew there were several possibilities. And hopefully whichever one ended up happening, it would lead to healing and a knowledge of where her next steps should lead. She knew it was way past time to get closure. And hopefully she would understand what she should end up putting in each of the three boxes on the floor so she could finally move forward with her life. It was time. She hugged the quilt one more time and laid it gently in the first box.

NANCY MACHLIS RECHTMAN

PURPLE AND AZURE

Once upon a time
I was the blonde little girl
Who loved to smile
And my hair was the color of sunshine
Until it gradually morphed into the hues of fallen leaves.
When the pieces of my world slowly fell away.

My memories have faded to sepia like old photographs
And I can no longer recognize who I was
Since I've lost the truth of who I am
I rely on my imagination to fill in the colors
 Of who I once might have been
In those days of sunshine and smiles.

In order to survive I've had to learn
That I need to paint inside the lines
And keep smiling
But now I think it's finally time
To break out of those constraints
And mix my own palette
Where maybe my hair is purple
And my skin sparkles like the azure sea
So I can stop depending on others to give me a name
But instead define who I am this time
And re-create me.

RUSSELL RICHARDSON

A GOON SQUAD IN THE RESTROOM

Rick was perched on the throne in the restroom when he saw a paperback copy of Jennifer Egan's *A Visit from the Goon Squad* on the floor beneath the next stall. The edge of the book touched against a stranger's pair of black Doc Martens. After a minute, the owner of the boots rose, flushed, and clomped away, banging the bathroom door behind him.

After finishing his own business, Rick hoisted his khakis and grabbed *Goon Squad* on his way out. Back in the candlelit glow of their table, he showed the book to his date, Janine. The paperback was, in the parlance of online merchants, *lightly used*. Almost *like new*. The spine showed just a hint of a crack. All four corners remained pointy.

"The guy in the next bathroom stall had it," Rick explained.

"You stole this?" asked Janine while examining the book in her hands. This was their third date, but Rick knew her well enough already to detect reproach.

"Of course not." Rick scowled and craned his neck to scan the restaurant. "The guy left it behind."

"But why take it?" She flipped to a page in the book, and her finger traced some text. "Actually, I heard good things about this. It won awards, I think."

"It raised a stir when it came out," said the distracted Rick. "That was years ago." He pointed at a far table, where two men sipped from wine glasses. "There. Those are the boots I saw."

Janine stretched for a better vantage, squinting against the dim light. They were adrift in a sea of tables, and the room was quite busy. "Are you sure? It's hard to see."

Snatching up the book, Rick rose from his chair. "I'll be back."

"Don't make a scene," cautioned Janine from behind, causing his shoulders to tense. He repeated her words under his breath, sourly, as he passed their server bringing their plates. Rick weaved through the dining room, muttering, "Make a scene? Why would she even say that? She doesn't know me at all!"

Rick reached the table, and the men looked up, expecting their waiter. "Hello?" asked the owner of the boots, a slight fellow who wore a silvery shirt and black jeans. A feathered earring hung from his left lobe. His partner had a perfectly trimmed goatee and big eyes that swelled behind gold-rimmed glasses.

"You forgot this in the bathroom," said Rick, setting the book on the table and expecting gratitude.

"That's not mine," said the man with a crooked smile. He swept one hand through his lustrous hair and, with the other, pushed back the paperback. The *Goon Squad* teetered on the edge before Rick caught it.

Rick stood for a moment, confused to be in possession of the book again. He bent to squint at the man's footwear and stood once more. "Those are your boots. This is your book. I was in the stall next to yours."

The man furrowed his brow at his companion and then gazed at Rick. "Sure, O.K. Fine. It was mine, but not now. I don't want it."

"Don't want it?"

"Yes, I left it for a reason. The book is boring."

"Boring?"

"Boring and repetitive, yes. The characters are unlikeable. I'd give it two stars for decent sentences, though. You know, *craft*."

Rick was flabbergasted. "You can't just leave stuff behind. That's littering."

The man in the boots leaned back with his wine glass cupped in his palm and chuckled. "I assumed someone else might want to read it. Maybe that's you."

"It's a bathroom, not a doctor's waiting room. Not a library!"

The men at the table stopped smiling. "What does it matter to you?" asked Mr. Boots, setting down his drink.

"You littered."

"I didn't."

"You did. You left something behind for someone else to pick up."

"I left it for someone else to *read*. That's different."

"So you're just made of money, then?" asked Rick. His voice had escalated, and other diners watched them now. "You can afford to buy a book and just discard it in a bathroom if it's boring? Must be nice."

"You should leave," said Mr. Boots, folding his arms.

Rick swiveled to the bearded guy, who looked like an underfed Sigmund Freud. "Do *you* condone littering?"

The man raised his hands as if protecting himself. "I didn't like the book, either."

Stunned, Rick thrust the *Goon Squad* forward for their inspection. "You two barely read it! The spine's not even cracked!"

"I had my *own* copy," snapped the bearded man.

"Oh? And where's yours?" asked Rick.

"Threw it away, as I recall."

"*Threw it away?* You people." Appalled, Rick turned back to the first man. "How can you fairly judge something you barely read?"

"I read enough," said Mr. Boots. "I skimmed. Now, won't you please leave?"

Their server appeared, showing concern. "*Monsieurs*, is there a problem?"

"Yes," said the bearded gentleman. "This person is harassing us."

"Ha-ha-harassing?" stammered Rick. He smacked the table, and the items upon it leaped and clattered. "These men are litterbugs!"

Mr. Boots broke into uncomfortable laughter. Incensed, Rick reached for his shirt collar, but the waiter grabbed his arm and, alarmed, Rick jerked and backhanded the waiter's face, throwing him into the table behind. The table collapsed under the waiter's weight, its diners dove for safety, and plates of food smashed on the floor.

Rick tried to apologize to the waiter and help him up, but was swatted him away. Other staff members were rushing over. Dinner, Rick saw, was over.

A few minutes later, Janine carried their coats through the front door. She threw his at Rick, which caught him by surprise, and it fell to the slushy sidewalk. He said nothing, knowing he was in no position to act offended.

"I've never been so embarrassed," she hissed.

"I'm sorry. Things got out of hand." After a pause, he shook his fist at the restaurant's wide front window and bellowed, "Big jerks! Stupid goons!"

After that, they stood on the corner without speaking, awaiting their Uber.

"Maybe you are meant to read the book," said Janine, nodding to the paperback in the crook of Rick's elbow. He could tell she was trying to be the better person. "The universe brought you together," she said.

"Actually, I read it when it came out," said Rick, flatly. He stared at the traffic that motored past.

"You did?" she asked. "Why didn't you say so? What did you think of it?"

"Eh. Pretty boring."

She gave him a long, hostile look.

"What?" asked Rick. He rolled his eyes. "O.K., I admit that I understand why he left it on the floor."

Janine took out her phone and began pressing icons on the screen.

"What are you doing?" he asked, sensing trouble.

"Getting an Uber for myself."

Rick's shoulders slumped. "Are we breaking up?"

Janine turned her back to him and remained that way until the first Uber arrived. Rick tried giving the book to her as a parting gift, but she stepped away from him, so he climbed into the car without saying goodbye.

The ride was quiet. Rick offered the book to the driver, who said that she didn't read, and weren't books dead? When Rick reached his apartment building, he left the paperback behind on the seat. He didn't need it, anyway. He still had a copy.

RUSSELL RICHARDSON

AGREE TO DISAGREE (WITH FEATHERS)

On Tom's wedding day, a cousin from out of town took him aside outside the church. "You need to know this, Tommy," said the cousin, a double divorcee. "Both parties bring a logical fallacy into a marriage. The man expects that the woman will never change. The woman expects that he will."

Tom pondered this for a moment, out of respect for the cousin who had flown across the country. The man patted the shoulder of Tom's tuxedo. "It's an old adage. For good reason."

Five years later, Tom and Claire received an invitation to that cousin's third wedding. By then, Tom had experienced enough of marriage to agree with the wisdom imparted by the cousin on the day of his nuptials. Tom had expected Claire to always be the care-free woman he had dated for three months, while she had mistakenly assumed wedlock would mature him and groused constantly about Tom's flaws.

Communication was a primary problem. Tom thought he understood her needs but often didn't, which led to bickering.

"I just need you to listen," she would say.

"I see," he would say, but rarely did.

They tried couples' counseling. The therapist was a woman who modeled herself after Sigmund Freud. Tom found her unlit cigar distracting and often responded with, "I'm sorry, what was the question?" and "Yeah, what she just said made, uh, a lot of sense. Off-topic, though, I wanted to say..."

After two sessions, Tom volunteered for overtime hours at work that conflicted with their appointment slot, and they never returned.

Claire's friend introduced them to *The Five Love Languages* and declared it a very insightful book. Tom learned that the dialects of love are:

a) Words of Affirmation
b) Quality Time
c) Physical Touch
d) Acts of Service
e) Receiving Gifts

"Those all sound nice," said Tom. "Who would have guessed there are only five?"

"But which one is specifically yours?" implored Claire.

"B . . . I guess," answered Tom, intently peering into the book as if he was reading a page but really just waiting to move on. "Although, E, too. Maybe."

She had declared what her language was, but he hadn't paid super close attention and forgot it ten minutes later. He didn't dare ask again, or she would be pissed.

Eventually, Tom learned that men were from . . . well, he couldn't recall. Were men from Mars, and women from Venus? Or vice-versa? Yes, men had to be from Mars, because the alliteration made for a more marketable title, he reasoned. But . . . maybe men came from Venus because it rhymed with penis? He would have to Google it again.

He and Claire were certainly from different planets. He kept his miseries to himself. She gave a full marital report to her entire social circle, which Tom knew about because she told him so. "All my friends agree . . ." she would say. And: "I discussed this with so-and-so . . ." And: "Perhaps I should poll my friends to see what they think about your behavior."

Tom began to dislike her friends. When he would cross paths with one, Tom could not refrain from thinking about all the private details that the friend, this *outsider*, knew about him. He preferred to be an open book with a couple of chapters redacted.

Claire forwarded to him a link from a friend to an NPR story about old couples that had persevered for decades. The idea of decades made Tom shudder. He skimmed the article and found one line repeated a few times: "Don't go to bed angry." But when else was Tom supposed to go to bed? It seemed like most of the old codgers benefited from hearing aids that they could turn off at will.

One week, they read *The Four Agreements* in bed while Tom felt sleepy and bored. When the book was finished, they shared their takeaways.

"Wasn't there a lot of padding in the book?" said Tom unhelpfully. "And aren't there only two agreements, really? If I am impeccable with my word, then aren't I doing my best? And if I don't make assumptions, then I won't take things personally, right?"

Propped up by pillows, Claire sat and stared at him.

"I'm just saying, there could be only two agreements. And they would fit on one side of a bookmark."

She continued staring.

"It would save a lot of time and money," he muttered to himself, trailing off and reaching for the lamp.

They arrived at *one* agreement, at least. They decided that a shared, central concern might strengthen their marriage—something like a child, but not a real child, that would be cruel. Tom suggested a pet, and she wanted a house. They stopped at a pet store on the way to a realtor's office.

Claire was allergic to cats, so that ruled out felines. Tom hated fish and reptiles and spiders: all the cold-blooded creatures that people think are capable of affection but aren't. He suggested a big dog, yet Claire preferred something tiny that made small poops. Then, they wandered into the bird department.

Parakeets, finches, and canaries ignited no passion in Tom or Claire. They felt neutral about cockatiels, although Tom really liked the word and couldn't stop repeating it under his breath, alternately accentuating the syllables. "COCK-a-tiel."

"Cock-AHH-tiel." "Cock-a-TIIIEEEELLL." Just like that, ad nauseam.

She was ready to kill him when they reached the parrots.

"Oh, he's beautiful," she remarked dreamily, touching the cage of a blue and gold Macaw. Tom saw the price sticker and barked with laughter. "It would be cheaper to buy a house," he said.

Claire didn't care. She had found what she wanted. The credit card was out, and the bird was hers.

On the way home, Claire rode with the cage in her lap in the passenger seat. Tom was struck by a thought he couldn't keep to himself and mused aloud, "There really is only *one* agreement. If I'm doing my best, then I'm not making assumptions. Forget a bookmark, put that on a button: *Do Your Best.* Four agreements, my foot!" He was relieved to see that Claire had been too enamored by her new friend to hear him.

She turned to Tom and said, "His name is Captain Seeds."

"O.K.," said Tom.

"Did you say something before?" she asked.

Over the next few weeks, Claire's attention and energy went into caring for Captain Seeds. The bird roamed freely through the apartment, and he spent the nights on a perch in the bedroom with them. Claire taught the bird to speak—at first just simple words, then building to small phrases.

"You're a beauty," she would say.

"You're a beauty," repeated the parrot.

"Only you understand me," said Claire.

"Only you understand me," parroted the Captain.

Soon, she talked more to the bird than she did to Tom. Claire would watch sitcoms with Captain Seeds, sitting on the couch beside her, and he would laugh whenever she laughed. If they watched a *Lifetime* movie, the parrot mimicked her crying, too, wiping his face with a gnarled, black foot.

Tom left town on a business trip for a few days, and when he returned, Captain Seeds had taken over his side of the bed, lying on Tom's pillow at night and sleeping beside Claire.

Tom didn't enjoy his time on the couch. Some nights, he was

awakened by a stray sunflower seed's shell that stabbed his side. In the mornings, his lower back would hurt, and he would have to tiptoe into the bedroom so as not to disturb the slumbering pair while he collected his work clothes. Eventually, he kept his clothes in a hamper in the spare bathroom and stopped going into his old room altogether.

The time came to leave for his cousin's wedding. Tom didn't mention anything to Claire or Captain Seeds, he simply packed a suitcase and left and never returned to the apartment.

RIE SHERIDAN ROSE

I WILL BURY MY LOVE IN TOPAZ

Some . . . many . . . will call my story mad. To claim a love as hot as the stars—that lasted merely seven days. They'll scoff, but those who doubt are wrong.

My poor village nestled on a hillside. Too far from the market road to receive traffic, and too close to the summit to encourage newcomers. My father was a blacksmith; my mother a baker. I was most often found on the hilltop with book in hand, sitting beneath my favorite tree.

That Moonday was no exception. My book had led me to another world, much brighter than my own. I was deep in its pages when a voice above me startled me back to reality.

"The writer must be a master indeed to coax you such a distance."

I jumped, dropping the book and losing my place. Looking up, I saw the most intriguing girl. She was dressed in filmy white, like the moon had come to earth—hardly the costume for climbing trees—and leaves twined in her hair. A moonstone hung about her neck.

"Shall I join you, or will you come up?" she queried, and my heart was hers. I know how ridiculous that sounds . . . but it doesn't make it false.

"I'll come up, if you please."

"Indeed I do." She patted the branch beside her and I scrambled up.

"I've never seen you before," I said, rather breathlessly. "Are you new to the village?"

Her eyes were silver as she gazed at me. "I've been here always."

"I'm Corwyn." I extended a hand, and she took it. Energy spiked through me—as if I had been grazed by lightning—and I almost fell from the tree. She steadied me, deceptively strong.

"My name is Elara. Show me your world."

And so it began.

The rest of Moonday passed in a blur. I didn't want to share her with the village, fearing censure and ridicule, so I showed her the rest of my world—the comforting wood nestling on the hill above us; the whispering brook that provided water and recreation; the crest of the hill with its broken crown. I showed her everything *but* the village.

As the sun began to sink, she sighed. "I must go."

"Will I see you again?" I cried in dismay, already bereft.

"Look for me at sunrise." She stepped away from me, and I gasped, as a pair of iridescent wings unfolded from her back and lifted her into the darkening sky.

Elara laughed. "You must learn to be more observant, my love," she teased. She blew me a kiss and darted away into the twilight.

I slept not a wink that night, my head filled with questions. Who was Elara? Goddess or sprite? Did she mean those last words? Did I return them?

The sun peeped in my window on Tiwesday, and I was out of the hut before anyone else awoke. My footsteps turned instinctively toward the tree where we'd met. My heart thundered in my ears— would she be there, or was it all a dream?

She waited beneath the tree. "Today, I'll show you *my* world," she said with a smile. Her gown was of shimmering red today, and a ruby hung about her neck. "Take my hand."

I did as she asked, and she lifted into the air. I gave a startled cry as my feet left the ground.

"You'll get used to it, beloved. Do not fear."

I gripped her hand tightly as we rose higher and higher. I could see people stirring in the village now. They looked so small and ordinary . . .

The things she showed me that day! A cavern deep inside the hillside with gleaming crystals embedded in its walls. A golden aspen grove, buried like a cathedral in the forest. Secret things I had never seen, though I had lived beside them all my life. By the end of the day, we were no longer flying, but walking hand in hand, lost in each other's eyes.

Elara looked tired. Carrying me about all day must have been draining.

"You should go rest, my dearest," I scolded her. "We'll speak more tomorrow."

She nodded, biting her lip. "You're right. Tomorrow, then."

Wodnesday, she dressed in purple, amethyst at her throat. Her dress matched the circles under her eyes.

We sat together under the tree, talking of our lives. She told me she was of the fay who dwelt within the wood. Spying me as I wandered there one day, she'd followed me home and vowed we should meet.

I told her of my secret dream to go away to study and make something of my life that didn't involve laboring over some sort of hot fire all day.

When the sun began to set, she flew away. I wondered if I'd see her again, as ill as she appeared.

But she was there next morning, dressed in sapphire, with matching pendant. I asked her about her jewels, and she explained how each related to a day of the week, and their significance.

Frigeday, she wore green, with an emerald. Most of the day, she napped upon my lap. I knew I was losing her, and it broke my heart.

On Saeternesday, I feared she wouldn't come, but she did. Her gown was the color of a cloudless sky, and her necklet of turquoise. Her face was wan—its sparkle of life leached away.

"I fear we'll not meet again, my dearest," she whispered. "Your world has drained me. I want you to have something to remember me by—or use to go away. Whatever you desire." She pressed a box into my hand. Within it tangled her pendants on their golden chains.

Hands trembling, she added the turquoise. "These are all I have to give you, except my love. That is yours eternally."

I kissed her then, for the first and last time. She slipped away in my arms.

Our love was brief . . . but beautiful. When she's safe within the sheltering ground, I'll take her final gift and leave this place. I'll make something of my life—spread her teaching about the stones and their properties.

My mother has a dress of butter yellow. Tonight, I'll dress Elara in it. Tomorrow, I'll place the topaz about her neck and bury her beneath our tree. Fitting for a Sunnanday.

RIE SHERIDAN ROSE

WALKING WITH HADES BY MOONLIGHT

Hell.
Yes, I know it is.
And yet, there is beauty here as well.

We walk in silence along the Lethe,
both with bated breath . . .
afraid to show a smile . . .

Here is perpetual moonlight—
But is the sun a necessity?
Cool twilight has its magic.

I learn of him.
He broods . . .
Who can blame him?

Reviled for dealing out Olympian punishment . . .

Lord of Midnight—
King of the Dead—

And, still, I find him gentle.

Mother would never understand.
There was no pressure.
No trick.

Just a shyly offered gift
and six seeds of compromise.

CASSANDRA O'SULLIVAN SACHAR

TRAPPED IN A STUDIO APARTMENT FOR ETERNITY

As Arthur stared out the window of the tiny apartment, he wondered, *Why did I have to die here, of all places?*

After attempting to leave through the door and via the window on multiple occasions only to be repelled back, he realized he was confined to this singular location: a dull, cramped studio apartment in Brooklyn, roughly 500 square feet, if his rough measurements and math were accurate.

He didn't have his cell phone on his person when he passed, so everything was only an estimate, and he had forgotten most of his math skills, having not used them in decades despite the empty promises of his junior high algebra teachers.

His ghostly form wouldn't move when he tried to stick his head or body out the door or window, passageways that led to anywhere else he could have spent his eternity.

He wished he had his phone. Could a ghost tap into Wi-Fi? If only he had a ghostly phone!

Maybe that would have given him a better idea of how to spend his spare time, a luxury that failed to exist when he was an actual breather, a man of flesh and blood who spent most of his hours working. Without access to Google or any handbook to the spiritual realm, he had no clue how to proceed. His future stretched out in front of him, an interminable road with nowhere to go.

While he could somehow perch on the couch rather than sink through it, as he could with walls and doors, Arthur had no method of touching anything else or contacting a creature in the living realm. He was a bystander, an invisible voyeur. It was confusing being trapped here with no purpose, it seemed, just a million unanswered questions.

Was this temporary? Would he flit away to another place some-day, a version of heaven or hell? He hadn't been particularly saintly or evil in life, so this seemed unlikely.

If the building burned down, heaven forbid, would he remain trapped in a cubicle of air? Would he meet other spectral residents?

And the main question: If one needed to remain in the walled space where one died, why couldn't he have perished in a cathedral? Back in his living days, as a single man with a decent income, he enjoyed traveling. He remembered the lofty ceiling and illuminated stained glass of Notre-Dame. He imagined that others must have expired there, as well, over hundreds of years of the cathedral's existence—a heart attack, or maybe a stroke. Had he died there, he might have met other cultured travelers who were worthy of a stimulating conversation every year or so. Maybe every decade—Arthur wasn't one for small talk.

But when he remembered being alive, Arthur couldn't help but recall how he died in Aunt Ethel's shabby apartment.

A kind woman who sent birthday cards with five-dollar bills from age one until fifty-three, the age at which he'd had his final birthday, Aunt Ethel loved her odd nephew and appreciated his monthly visits despite the stilted conversation.

He remembered the saccharine, chemical taste of the candy. She was always forcing the damned things on him. He had accepted to be polite. The price he paid for his manners!

It revolted him, and he desperately desired to spit it out, yet he dared not behave in such a crass way. He sucked for a while, trying to make it minuscule enough to pass down his gullet. Arthur wanted to rid his mouth of that awful taste.

But it hadn't shrunk enough to swallow and thus lodged in his throat. He realized he was in trouble and tried to cough it out. When that failed, he attempted the Heimlich maneuver on himself on the back of a chair. In his panic, his technique left much to be desired.

Aunt Ethel screamed and wailed, hitting him in what she

thought was his diaphragm.

But it was too late.

Then, suddenly, Arthur was staring at himself, prone and lifeless on the floor. He felt fine, far from the agony of mere moments before, but it soon became apparent that he was *not* fine. Far from it.

Poor Aunt Ethel. He observed her as she dealt with the aftermath of his death: the look of horror on her face as she shook his lifeless body, the gut-wrenching sobs while she called 9-1-1, her bloodshot eyes when the paramedics carted him out.

Her guilt was so severe that she moved out, denying him the comfort of a familiar, if not close, companion. He would never know what became of her other than that she went to a senior citizen living facility, which he learned from overhearing her on the phone.

Aunt Ethel left, but Arthur remained trapped in this minuscule apartment in the same light blue sweater with fraying sleeves. Once, years before the fateful day on which he unknowingly selected this final outfit, his co-worker Susan had mentioned that it brought out his eyes. After spilling these words, she flushed bright pink and walked away.

The sweater became his favorite after that, and he wondered what would have happened if he had made more of an effort. Shy Susan with her wild mane of hair and parade of cardigan sweaters, buttoned all the way up to her throat, had intrigued him. What if he'd had the courage to invite her for a coffee?

It was another "what if" in the life that was no longer his, a quiet, solitary existence with missed opportunities. Too much of an introvert to feel comfortable attending a company happy hour, Arthur's Friday nights usually involved treating himself to a single finger of whiskey while watching a World War II documentary, or, if he really wanted to unwind, he might pour himself a cognac and listen to NPR in his study, looking out the window at the Manhattan skyline. He was fortunate to have invested well in his youth, so he had splurged, buying an apartment with this breathtaking amenity.

It might have been nice to share that fabulous view with someone else.

But it was too late.

All he had was his afterlife now. The fraying sleeve would never worsen—he had tried to pull the yarn to see what would happen, but it sprang back, completely unharmed. Likewise, the crinkles around his eyes would never deepen, nor would the gray creep up and overtake his light brown hair. Like his sweater, he was stuck in time, never to change, a middle-aged man for eternity.

At times he'd rummage through his wallet just to feel something in his hand and remind himself that he had once been a living man who drove a car and used credit cards. In his pocket when he died, his wallet had traveled with him to the afterlife.

Arthur wished he could retrieve the books in his study, items likely boxed up and sold at a thrift shop by now. How he would love to read the complete works of Shakespeare, Dickens, and Austen. He was quite well-read but had not read everything.

Now, with an ocean of time. he had no access to those masterpieces. He'd even attempt to read a romance novel, a cringe-worthy Danielle Steel or Nicholas Sparks if he could get his hands on one, but there were no options.

After Aunt Ethel moved out, a man named Gerald moved in. A fortyish, unkempt slob, Gerald worked from home as an automobile insurance agent.

Gerald gave minimal effort to this career. With little else to occupy his time, Arthur quickly memorized Gerald's pitch and would yell feedback to him to increase his sales, but, as always, it remained unheard.

Unambitious, Gerald remained disinterested in becoming promoted or earning employee of the month. He clocked his hours, and, when completed, focused on his real passions: video games and pornography.

These pastimes were equally repugnant in terms of Gerald's actions and sounds. Once the headset went on or a certain type of music played, Arthur knew it was time to give Gerald space.

Sadly, there was nowhere to go. Perhaps Arthur *was* in hell, after all.

Arthur's entertainment mostly consisted of looking out the window to avoid seeing Gerald scratch himself all day. There was nothing he could do to block out the incessant sound of Gerald's grating voice or the death metal "music" he blasted.

It was only on rare occasions, it seemed, when he was low on Miller Lite, Mountain Dew, and pork rinds, his staple groceries, that Gerald left the apartment and provided Arthur with some much-needed alone time. He would have preferred to watch a program or listen to a CD, maybe The Beatles or David Bowie, or, perhaps, some classical music, but silence was preferable to Gerald's noise.

Luckily, at least in Arthur's experience, ghosts couldn't smell. Gerald's diet of fried food and Domino's pizza made him produce copious sounds which Arthur imagined to be accompanied by fetid odors from which he was blessedly spared. Arthur's repeated cries for Gerald to take better care of himself were in vain.

And the state of the apartment! Gerald seemed to revel in his own filth, often forgetting trash day and allowing his takeout rubbish to pile up into a Leaning Tower of Pizza Boxes. Gerald threw can after can in the trash, not recycling.

It was *sickening*. He didn't even own a broom.

If he could, Arthur would have happily helped with the apartment upkeep, but none of his efforts were successful.

It was all quite dull, really, but it was his reality.

Thank goodness for the window. It wasn't quite the Manhattan skyline, but it was *something*, an escape from this studio apartment imprisonment.

While the window, this portal to a different world, faced a seedy liquor store that serviced a great number of neighborhood degenerates, he could view the sky in the morn-ing, day, dusk, and night, and thus observe nature's wonder as the sky metamorphosed. He watched as winter shed her icy cloak to make way for joyous rebirth in spring, saw fireflies blink their cheerful fairy lights in summer, beheld the leaves on the lone tree in his sight transform to brilliant colors and descend to the ground in autumn, and rejoiced when the first snowflakes fell, purifying the dirty street in a blanket of fresh snow.

This window allowed him to see life in his death.

*

Once, out of curiosity and boredom, Arthur tried to meld himself into Gerald to see if possession were possible. While the thought of *being* Gerald repulsed him, he longed for the simple pleasures of using the remote control or opening a book. Not that there were any books here, but he could order some if he had the power to touch a computer or phone.

It didn't work, and Arthur felt inappropriate for having tried.

*

Several years into Arthur's afterlife, Gerald showed up one day with a dog, a great mammoth of an adult German Shepherd.

It was completely unexpected; he hadn't gleaned a hint of this before it happened. In general, Arthur attempted to respect Gerald's privacy, as well as his own need for personal space, by not snooping at his text messages. Whenever anything seemed private, Arthur left Gerald do his thing, however abhorrent it might be, such as leaving the bathroom door completely open when he did his business.

In Gerald's defense, he didn't realize he had company.

But Arthur couldn't help but overhear his phone calls. Except for the work calls, they were few and far between.

When this lumbering oaf of a dog ambled into the apartment, Arthur's first thought was that everything would be so much dirtier than it already was.

Dogs were disgusting creatures, shedding hair, ruining furniture, and making messes. This dog might even be worse than Gerald.

He soon discovered that the dog was called Roger, a name more often yelled than spoken. Arthur pieced the clues together from words Gerald screamed into his headset as he played his video games. Roger had belonged to Gerald's brother, and now Gerald had to take him . . . something about separating from the wife and moving to an apartment that couldn't take dogs, maybe?

Poor Roger, abandoned by both of his humans, now to reside with the delinquent Gerald, a man barely able to care for himself. No wonder Roger kept his tail down and sighed throughout the night.

Arthur wanted to help this depressed dog, to comfort him in this difficult time. He remembered reading an article about animals being able to see the dead, so he tried to make his presence known.

He failed. Roger was as aware of Arthur as he was of the symbolism of the green light in *The Great Gatsby*—not at all. It was a myth, apparently, that living animals could perceive ghosts.

At least Gerald bought Roger tennis balls and what appeared to be the proper food. He didn't take the dog outside enough and raged when Roger made a mess, but Arthur felt that was Gerald's fault, not Roger's. Twice a day wasn't enough for a human, so how could it suffice for a dog?

With nothing else to do, against his own wishes, Arthur mentally clocked Gerald's bathroom visits at an average of eleven times per day. How was it fair to take Roger out only twice?

But Roger seemed to thrive outside. If Arthur was lucky, Gerald would take the German Shepherd to the small patch of grass and tree by the liquor store. Arthur smiled as he watched the serious dog take joy in his life, jumping with his two front paws on the tree or sniffing the trail of a mysterious, now departed animal.

Gerald always looked bored and pulled on the leash, eager to go back inside. The "walk" usually lasted all of ten minutes.

Arthur hoped Roger's previous owners had shown more enthusiasm, but, then again, they were willing to part with him. Why would one leave one's companion?

*

Time passed, as it does. Roger appeared hopeful every day, treating Gerald as a god, forever approaching his master with a tennis ball in his mouth. Roger would chew and ceremoniously plop the ball in front of Gerald, waiting for a throw, but Gerald usually ignored him. Eventually, Roger would give up.

Once in a hundred times, Gerald would throw the slimy mass across the room, swearing while he did. Happy for even a shred of attention, Roger would run like a maniac to fetch it, rarely rewarded with a second toss.

As if a dog's saliva was more disgusting than Gerald's menagerie of filthy habits. As if Gerald had a reason for depriving a simple pleasure to this poor, broken animal.

How Arthur longed to toss Roger that ball, to give attention to this lonely creature.

*

One night, after repeatedly being ignored, Roger slunk off to chew his ball.

Gerald was busy—headset on, f-words aplenty—engaged with his "gamer" community.

After several Miller Lites, Gerald passed out on the couch. He forgot to take Roger outside, so the German Shepherd stayed on the floor, chewing away, at least somewhat content.

In the silence, Arthur heard a wretched sound, a squeaking, whistling noise.

It was Roger. The ball was stuck in his throat. Arthur could see it still, lodged there—Roger hadn't swallowed it, thank God, but he was struggling, gasping for air.

The whistling increased. Arthur watched helplessly as Roger tried to expel the offending object.

He coughed. He gagged.

Arthur rushed to Roger and tried to pull the ball out, but his hand went right through it, as it always did with objects in the living world.

Arthur screamed at Gerald to wake up, roared at him, but it was useless. He simply couldn't make himself heard.

Finally, Roger shuddered and lay still.

Arthur felt hot tears streaming down his face. He didn't know his ghostly self was capable of even producing tears—after all, he didn't have any other bodily functions and couldn't sense heat or cold, always dapper in his blue sweater while Gerald sweated buckets in ratty old tee-shirts and boxers.

Were these really tears? He had never cried as a ghost before, and he couldn't remember when he had last felt such strong emotion even in life.

And then he felt something else.

A cold, wet touch on his hand, a sensation he had seldom experienced in life and never in death.

He looked down. There, to the left of his now vacant body, Roger stood in his brand-new ghostly form, licking Arthur's hand.

Roger cocked his head at Arthur, questioning.

Arthur reached out to place his hand on Roger's head and caress his coarse fur. As he scratched around his ears, Roger's tongue lolled out the side of his mouth. He grinned at this new human, and he leaned in, close.

Indeed, Roger seemed to adjust easily to this ghostly existence and looked nonchalant about his own corpse beside him.

Arthur, already squatting, reached out to the now sitting dog, drawing him into a hug.

"You're a good boy," he tried, having very few encounters with animals. "You're safe with me now."

Roger felt solid, substantial, and warm in Arthur's arms. He knew that Roger's literal heart was no longer beating, but he was pretty sure he heard the rhythm of a ghost heart. He couldn't remember, even in life, the last time he had embraced or been embraced, the last time he had been close enough, if ever, to hear a heartbeat.

Tears pricked his eyes for the second time that night.

Gerald snored away on the couch, unaware of the tragedy he would unearth when he woke. Maybe Gerald wasn't the best dog owner, but he cared about Roger in his own lazy way. Arthur dreaded witnessing the discovery.

Yet now *Arthur* was Roger's person, a fact the dog seemed to understand. He ignored his living, sleeping master and looked with devotion at his dead one, as if he knew he and Gerald were no longer existing on the same plane.

Still, Arthur worried. Would Roger be content trapped in here with him, no longer able to chase squirrels up trees or bask in the sun? While Roger had spent little time outdoors, at least in his tenure with Gerald, Arthur knew he adored those fleeting moments; he had seen it all from the window. Would Roger understand that his new master couldn't provide him with outings, food, and toys? What else did dogs desire if not those things?

He had never owned a dog, or any pet for that matter. He didn't know what to *do* to make a dog happy.

He pondered this as he stroked Roger's head. While the dog seemed a worthy companion, would this new development make Arthur's afterlife more complicated? Would he make this poor dog miserable? Arthur didn't want to disappoint him.

Roger wandered away, seemingly already tired of Arthur.

"Sorry, buddy, you're stuck with me, and there's not much to do here."

And then he felt it, a gentle touch on his foot. He looked down to see a tennis ball.

He picked it up, feeling the sliminess.

Of course! Just as Arthur had entered death with his wallet, Roger entered with his ball. A quick glimpse of the poor dog's corpse solidified the knowledge that Roger had died with the tennis ball in his mouth. While it failed to dislodge in life, it had slid out in death.

A grin on his face, Arthur threw the ball across the room. Roger took off like a shot, retrieving the ball and delivering it to Arthur's feet.

Arthur stared into the deep brown eyes. "I love you, Roger," he said.

It was the first time he had ever uttered those words.

"You're such a good boy." He drew Roger in for another hug. Roger licked Arthur right on his face.

An eternity in this apartment suddenly felt much more bearable.

*

Gerald's grief was short-lived. While surprised at the outcome, he failed to show much sadness.

He brought home a snake within a week.

Arthur wondered, *Would a snake become a ghost?*

He looked back at Roger, who also seemed skeptical.

They hoped not.

CASSANDRA O'SULLIVAN SACHAR

UPON LOSS

On the day my dad died, I was attending a writing research conference in Norway, sitting in a presentation about how to improve university composition programs. The Danish scholar showed a slide with a breakdown of feedback analysis—how he had coded different comments on the macro, meso, and micro levels.

Having presented my own research study on feedback the day before, I found it both relevant and interesting. A model conference attendee, I refrained from using my phone during presentations, but I wanted a photo of the slide for reference purposes.

As I opened the home screen to access the camera app, the text from my mom came through: My dad was gone, his suffering over.

The scholar continued presenting his data as my world caved in. A cold shiver ran through my body, and I knitted my fingers together to quell the quaking in my arms. Tears streamed down my face; I had no control over these visceral reactions. Somehow, I managed to remain quiet, containing the keening wail intensifying inside me.

From my place in the second row, I was loath to run out of the room—I have never been one to make a scene. So I stayed put, struggling to compose myself as the wave of emotions fought to pull me under.

Only a few days prior, on a Thursday, we had learned that my father was riddled with cancer: liver and bone to accompany the prostate cancer which he had previously vanquished, only to return again. My mother told me the PET scan of his liver was like a Lite Brite toy with everything glowing; to my sister, she said it looked like a beehive full of angry bees.

By the time we found out about the cancer trifecta, it was too late for treatment. He only made it to Tuesday morning in Norwegian time, just before midnight Monday night in America.

None of this was completely out of left field. He'd been hospitalized for nearly a month before the new diagnoses, full of pain after back surgery. Apparently, the reason his back hurt so much was because the cancer had begun consuming his spine, disintegrating his bones. But the surgeons didn't know at that time, and they forged ahead anyway. During the final month of his life, as he slipped in and out of delirium, he was in agony.

I've never been comfortable with death. Whenever a friend lost a parent, my heart went out to them, but I never knew what to say. I couldn't possibly understand what they were going through, and I worried that my words wouldn't carry enough weight or sympathy.

So this *is how it feels.*

As it turns out, it's not the words themselves that matter—it's that someone cares about you enough to say something, anything, as they see you going through it.

I know that now.

And I knew my father *would* die, that he had only days to weeks to live, that he might be gone before I returned from Norway. I visited the hospital right before the airport knowing I might never see him again, understanding that the shrunken man lying prone in the bed would never come home. He would never again send me cat memes, tell me a story I'd heard ten times before, or state how proud he was of me. We'd never watch a movie together while drinking our respective black coffees; we'd never spend far too much time analyzing an episode of a TV show we both loved. No more Thanksgivings, Christmases, or birthdays; no more playing Scattergories and playfully arguing that he was cheating, that his ridiculous answers didn't count.

As I left his hospital room, I told him I loved him and that I'd come see him again if he was still there when I returned. I said I understood if he had to leave, though. I saw the pain etched on his face. Every moment was torture for him.

I never saw him again.

*

When the conference session finished, I hightailed it back to my hotel room and finally allowed myself to fall apart. But my university had partially funded my trip, so I couldn't cry in my hotel room all day.

On the day my dad died, I attended other presentations, had lunch with a member of my dissertation committee whom I hadn't seen in ten years but who happened to be at the conference, and made several trips to my hotel room when I could no longer compartmentalize. Like the boiler in the Overlook Hotel in *The Shining*, the pressure inside me kept building. I could only keep myself from exploding by relieving the grief every so often, setting free the body-racking sobs like dangerous, wild animals released from their cages.

And so it went as the days and weeks continued after I flew home to a life without my father. The days without him stretched on, and I went about my business: teaching classes, grading papers, working with students during office hours, attending meetings, and completing my MFA coursework. I smiled and acted perky and met my deadlines and dissolved into a gooey mess in private at the drop of a hat.

I know how lucky I was to have him as a father. Before I had eight, our family moved twice because of his job. When he was transferred yet again, he commuted four hours a day for at least a year so as not to disrupt my family, choosing our convenience over his own.

He was one of the smartest people I have ever known. As a child, I spent many bedtimes listening to him recite Greek myths and tales from *1,001 Arabian Nights* from memory, effortlessly pulling forth the details to transport me across space and time. In adulthood, I leaned on him heavily for several research studies; he was my stats guy, dusting off textbooks from his graduate studies from decades earlier to help me support the efficacy of my writing interventions with quantitative data.

To this day, almost a year later, grief continues to surprise me, sneaking up on me when I least expect it. David Bowie's "Let's Dance" will come on the radio, and I'll remember how my dad would dance in the cringiest way possible whenever his phone would ring since that was, at one point, his ringtone. I'll call my mom's landline, and, even after I realize she's not picking up, I'll let the whole answering machine message play to hear my dad's voice—she never changed it. When I visit my mother, I pause as I walk by his favorite chair, wishing he was still in it. At first, I couldn't even walk into the living room—I couldn't bear seeing his empty chair.

A friend bought me a windchime as a bereavement gift. My husband hung it from a tree in the back yard. We like to sit outside in the warmer months, listening to music at dusk and drinking a glass of wine. When the wind blows and the chime tinkles, my husband says, "That's your dad saying hello." Fanciful, yes, but comforting nonetheless.

Just a few nights ago, I had a dream about my dad. The dream itself was inconsequential—we were sitting at a table together watching a tiny pet pig run around. Random.

But then the alarm went off, and my husband told me he had dreamt of my dad, too. Later that morning, I received a text from my daughter saying, "Had another Grandpa dream."

In one single night, he visited all of us. Or, if he didn't—if there was nothing mystical about it—our strong, loving memories of him brought some part of him to us.

And so it goes. We love, and we lose, but we never forget those who have helped shape our lives.

STEVE ZISSON

BRUCE

The newly mated pair of eastern coyotes is trotting toward the creek way at the back of my property. They bound up out of the long, late summer grass every few strides, yipping and yapping and trying to spot prey on each leap above the seed heads.

I'm nodding in awe at the sight of them as I talk on the phone, just a bit distracted.

"Everything's perfectly safe, Marie. It's foolproof. I've got a state-of-the-art electric fence. She'll love it," I tell my ex-wife as I look out from my kitchen window across my newly re-imagined backyard landscape.

She says she'll have to think about it after she gets more data and she hangs up abruptly. All hang-ups come without warning from Marie.

Still, I sense softening. I've made some progress with my ex-wife to allow our daughter to come to my house. Marie will be sending a drone to do a week's worth of surveillance, day and night, just to make sure it's safe. I'm okay with that. Science is observation.

Once the hurdle of her mother is cleared, I'm sure Ames will love it here. She's a real nature lover. Even Marie might like it, stay for a while, though she's an avowed city person. I thought we would've balanced each other out when we got married. But I guess we were too far apart. City and country. Nature seeks a balance but we couldn't find it.

She needs the city and person-to-person contact. My research and I can work anywhere.

My backyard is almost a back forty acres, widening out from my farmhouse positioned near the road. My neighbors aren't really thrilled with what I'm doing with the backyard. The town's approved it up until now so the neighbors can just take me to court.

I should sketch a hand-drawn map of the backyard and send a copy to Ames. She'll love it and she'll want to come *all* the time. She used to stay over every other weekend until my backyard went wild. Until I encouraged the wilding. I did it mostly for her because I knew she couldn't resist being here more.

But Marie, of course, didn't see it that way. She thinks my backyard is dangerous and so anti-city. Cities are the future, she says, so confidently as a city planner in Boston. A city that was never planned and sprouted randomly along winding cow paths.

The two coyotes stop in mid-frolic and I scan the area to spot what froze them. A young deer is the proverbial deer in the headlights. Breakfast, lunch, and dinner for hungry coyotes.

I revel in the beauty of the coyotes out in daytime, not confined to the night hours like they are in urban environments, where they avoid us to hunt.

The deer and the coyotes stare each other down and the greyer coyote crouches and begins to circle until it's behind the deer, staring at its puffy white tail.

The deer is motionless. It eyes the tan coyote still in front of it. It needs eyes on its rear too.

The grey coyote lunges at its tail and comes away with a mouthful of white fur. It furiously spits it out.

The deer whirls around so its rear faces the second coyote.

As if infuriated by the near miss, the coyote with the mouthful goes for the neck but the deer lowers its head and butts him away. The coyote tumbles into a bush before righting itself. The deer drops its head again for another charge but the coyote at the rear takes the opening and dives in, burying its jaw into its anus. And it holds on as the deer whips around and around. Blood leaks from a tear in its rear and is wicked up by its flicking white tail as if it's a cotton ball.

Should I stop the carnage? No. All must be as natural as possible in my backyard.

*

The next morning I find the deer carcass, just bones and fur and blood stains in the matted grass where the coyotes alternately gorged and slept with their meal.

Such is the circle of life in my new backyard. It feels so alive. I won't protect Ames from seeing any of it. She already loves animals and nature shows and ecosystems. She certainly understands how a key predator can cause a trophic cascade. She informed me what a trophic cascade was just last year!

I take another sip from my coffee thermos even as I realize my bladder's full. I look around to check if a neighbor can see me as I unzip. It's a vulnerable position and I'm far from a neighbor but Tremblay spies on me with a telescope. He's got a drone too but he knows not to violate my backyard airspace.

Stepping behind a scrub pine, I crouch and let it all out. Tremblay would charge me with indecent exposure if he spotted me. On my own property! Tremblay of perfect lawn who hates my backyard, demanding that I mow it. He's complained to the town about it a hundred times.

The Conservation Commission has been out for a half dozen site visits as have the police. The ConCom has mostly been concerned about the creek that has grown in width, depth and saltiness as the ocean, almost three miles away has pushed the brackish water west of my property. And all kinds of sea creatures have ventured to my backyard where I've built a small creek-side beach.

First come the herring in the spring and behind them even a couple of lost Atlantic Salmon. Larger predators to follow.

Ames will just love the beach. I had to truck in sand because so much gets washed away each flood tide. The sand is tan, local sand, not bleached bright white like it was from the Caribbean.

I head down to the beach to see what's washed up or washed away. I've worn a path to the beach and there's a wind blowing up the creek pushing a strong thick salt sting into my nose. But it's more than that as I approach. It's a salty thickness in the air. A big black lump half out of the water is the source of the stench. Herring gulls and crows and crabs scramble over it, pecking away at the flesh.

I've got to get it removed now. Marie won't like the look of it. Whatever it is, I'm sure it's not going to be easy. It's a leaden lump of hundreds of pounds of dead weight.

I feel another presence from above and it's a drone. It must be Marie's and not Tremblay's. She's already probably seen the carcass on her feed so the chance that Ames can come is evaporating.

Shit, it smells like . . . shit. Is it a dead seal? None of the horseheads have ever come this far up the creek. But they do like to haul out their nine-hundred pounds on beaches to rest and avoid great whites.

I scan the water for a fin. Marie won't ever let Ames come if her drone spies a great white shark.

The drone peels off down the creek toward the sea. Returning my attention to the rotting mound of blubber, I watch as the swarm of crabs and insistent squawking crows jockey for position. Something huge must have taken off this gray horsehead seal's head. Something very big. A boat propeller?

It'll be a long time before the crabs and coyotes and crows and turkey vultures eat through that much flesh. I will return with my tractor to push it back into the creek, flushing it out to sea on the high tide.

*

The next morning, I drive the John Deere to the beach and not much stink greets me as I crest the dune.

The carcass is gone. Not a scrap left. No crabs or crows either. The overnight tide wasn't unusually high so something must have dragged it away.

I look for drag marks but it's like the sand has been raked smooth by a gentle tide. Nine-hundred pounds just vanished.

The neat look of the beach makes me think of my long-term plan of building a marsh as a buffer from storms. Ames would love to help with the planning. As I'm daydreaming, another drone hovers above me and then over the spot the seal was, before it's zipping north up the creek.

*

Ames is coming! I've got to get ready and make everything perfect!

Can nature be perfect? A perfect balance? Is it achievable? Maybe in my backyard. Maybe not in your backyard.

Ames will never want to leave.

Ames is perfect at age twelve but so different as I see her for the first time in six months. Stepping out of the shuttle with just a weekend bag, she seems to have sprouted six inches, her dark hair a foot longer too, down to the small of her back. Can she stay longer than her little bag portends? I will get her anything she needs, to keep her with me as long as possible.

I bounce down the porch like a big dog, arms and legs flailing.

"I miss this porch!" she says, hugging me. "And you too, Pauline, I mean, Mom, of course. I could sit in this very spot all afternoon with a book."

"I've got so much more to show you. It's all for you," I whisper into her hair. "It's out back. I've built a new porch off the kitchen for viewing. You can read there afternoons if you can keep your eyes off the landscape."

We stop in the kitchen just long enough for Ames to toss her bag on the island and grab a couple lemonades.

On the back porch I can see Ames eyes widen as she slugs down her lemonade.

"I was so thirsty! There's no green lawn anymore!"

"Isn't it beautiful? So brown."

"And long."

I take her glass and mine and put them on the grill. "I've got a big surprise for you. Let's go down the path to the creek."

She's off the porch before me and it's so hot I can't wait to show her the beach. And maybe go in for a dip. Two drones zip in from the left and right of my property. Are both Marie's? Or is one Tremblay's?

She's skipping ahead like a young coyote on her own for the first time. How can she ever leave and go back to the city?

She's over the hill before the path plunges toward the creek in its little valley and I'm running after her to make sure there's nothing out of the ordinary, like a big dead animal, or even something dangerous.

And she's yelling, screeching before I can emerge from the marsh reeds blocking my view.

She's alone when I finally spot her near where the seal beached itself or floated there already dead. "Look what I found!"

It glints in the sun at me. "What . . . is . . . it?" I ask, out of breath.

"It's a tooth. A big one."

I'm still catching my breath as I reach her.

"It's huge," she says, holding it up to me. "I think it's a shark's tooth. A very big one."

"Let me see," I say, holding out my hand.

It has the shape of a shark's tooth. Triangular, and the edges are serrated. For cutting hunks of flesh. Efficiently. It looks like an arrowhead.

I flip it over a couple times in my hand, which it almost fills. "It seems like it's fake or something. A hard plastic. Like it was made."

"Like it didn't come from nature? We could get it tested, couldn't we?"

I study it closer. Definitely feels like plastic but also alive. "We could. But for right now, you've got a great keepsake. We'll mount it and hang it on the wall in your room." To help keep her here.

Ames smiles so wide that I know she'll stay forever. Her visit couldn't be going any better.

*

Ames comes down for breakfast, all bleary-eyed. She's in shorts and her Dinosaur Jr. band T-shirt I gave her. She's holding the shark tooth with two hands above her head like she's a priest raising it to the heavens. "I was doing some research. All night really. It's got to be a megalodon tooth!"

"Around the Cape? No one's found their teeth in Massachusetts waters before."

"Maybe it was brought up on the Gulf Stream. The current's getting so much stronger every day as the ice sheet melts. It's pulling stuff right up off the ocean floor."

She does do her research.

"I've made you a vegan breakfast sandwich. Just like you like," I say, holding out a plate.

"Great," she says, lunging for it. She doesn't take a bite though. "Let's wrap it up and take it with us on the kayak. I want to explore down the creek."

"I don't know Ames. We should get the drone up first to take a look. I didn't tell you about—"

She's digging in the kitchen drawer for aluminum foil and rips off a sheet with a metal-on-metal fingernails on blackboard sound. "Didn't tell me what, Mom?"

"I didn't tell you about the huge dead seal I found on the beach the other day. It had a big bite out of it."

"Could've been hit by a boat."

I point to the tooth on the countertop. "This was no boat."

"But we've been kayaking a million times on the creek and open ocean. We'll have the drone out in front of us to see if anything is coming our way."

I can't disappoint her if I want her to keep coming back. To stay. More than a weekend.

*

We're in our two-person kayak and at least it's a cloudy day so the morning sun isn't beating down on us. We're not much past Tremblay's frontage but the creek is already widening and deepening as we approach the ocean.

"Real shark's teeth are made of calcium phosphate," Ames says from behind me. She's still in research mode while also operating the drone. I'm the muscle, paddling against the current as the tide swells into our creek. The water's clear enough that I can see schoolie stripers foraging for crabs and bait fish.

"Full disclosure, Ames. I did see a mako shark swimming up the creek a few weeks ago. I couldn't believe it. Following the stripers. Makos aren't as dangerous as great whites. But—"

"There's a boat coming, Mom. Fast!" Ames says.

It's got to be that asshole Tremblay in his cigarette boat. Steaming up the creek like he's some president Bush on a fast ride off Kennebunkport. Or thinking he's in *Miami Vice*.

Before I can pull out of the channel over to the creek side, he's churning past us not ten feet away. The wake rocks us over almost one way and then the other on the return but we seem to right ourselves. And I'm yelling at him but I'm sure he can't hear us over his dual outboard engines.

He circles us and the second wake flips us. I'm flailing and out of the kayak, trying instinctively to find Ames.

The first time I surface I see the two drones. Ames will never be allowed back is all I can think for a second. Marie'll have it all on video.

No Ames in sight. I dive again.

When I come up, I spot Ames swimming back to the kayak and a shark fin not twenty yards behind her. It's as big as a boat's sail from water level. And it's gaining on her.

There's nothing I can do. Just watch.

And I'm amazed as the fin goes right past her, headed toward Tremblay's boat.

Even if the water were murky, you couldn't miss how huge this thing is. It's at least twice the length of the kayak, maybe thirty feet. It fills the creek, a dark shadow under the water, creating its own wake above. A wave rushes toward Tremblay's boat that he's backing up to dock at his pier.

Two drones pause over us and then head toward the shark and Tremblay.

"Ames, hurry," I say and we swim the kayak to shore, each of us hanging onto a side.

As we stand up in knee deep water near the bank, the shark rises up next to Tremblay's boat. It looks almost mechanical in weird slow motion. Its open jaws crash onto the stern and take off the back of the boat. Tremblay goes skyward, lands, and slides toward the hole in the back headed for the snapping jaws and shark eyes rolling back in its head.

"He should've gotten a bigger boat and not a fast flashy one," I mutter to myself.

"What?" Ames asks.

"Nothing."

I grab Ames and turn her away when the shark's bite severs Tremblay's body in half, the blood draining out of him and into the creek.

I can't help but gasp but think to pull Ames up onto the marsh grass for good measure in case the shark turns to us next.

But the shark is busy, thrashing Tremblay's fiberglass boat into so many pieces.

*

We're only a hundred yards up the path toward home when Marie calls, as expected.

"I'm all right Mom. You should have seen it. It was massive," Ames says to her. "I know you saw it. But from a drone. We were in the water with it!"

I'm proud that Ames is unfazed. I probably could've let her watch Tremblay succumb but it probably would be too much for anyone. Poor Tremblay. I wouldn't wish that death on my worst enemy. It was quick at least. He wasn't my worst enemy, just maybe a bitter rival.

"No Mom," Ames says calmly, like a scientist I know she'll become. "There'll be an investigation and all. A man is dead! I'll have to stay for a few days. And we have to find out more about this mega shark.

Ames looks over to me and I can see her excitement in her nodding eyes. She's going to be staying a few more days!

The swampy ground never felt so solid under my feet.

As we walk toward the house, Tremblay's Pitbull mix howls from his property like he's sensed the loss of his owner. I never really took to that dog but I feel for him now.

*

"Mom says you did a good job getting me out of the water."

"She did?"

"She did."

Maybe there's hope after all.

We're sitting on the back porch and Ames is reviewing the drone footage.

"Look at this! It's not a long lost megalodon," she says. "It's Bruce."

"Bruce who?"

She brings over her screen to me. "No silly, the shark is Bruce."

She's always giving wild animals names. Like the abandoned baby squirrel she found that time. Or the opossum.

"The shark?"

She sits in close to me and pulls up a split screen. "It's what Spielberg named the mechanical sharks he built for his *Jaws* movie. He named them Bruce. Look, they're the same."

"What?"

Damn, they do look similar though the one in the water looked so much more real when it was right next to you.

"Wow. I remember when they filmed that movie over on the Vineyard. Robert Shaw starred in it. Dreyfus and that other guy, Schneider. Roy I think. I loved that movie but I never understood why anyone could be scared by that fake-looking shark."

"Scheider, not Schneider. There's no 'n' in his name," Ames corrects me, then quickly moves on and points to our drone footage. "This one definitely looks more shark-like. Like it's adapted to nature. Spielberg built a half dozen of them but four or five just disappeared like movie props sometimes do. One was displayed at Universal Studios for a while."

My eyes go wide. I'm buying into her thinking. Sometimes we get like this with wild theories. Science often springs from out-there theories. "Maybe they just dumped the mechanical sharks in the ocean like they did everything else in the 70s," I say.

"And real great white sharks used Bruce as an enhancement!"

"As if great whites need any enhancement."

"I don't think a typical great white could do what Bruce did to Mr. Tremblay and his boat. It's something beyond the usual."

We both sit back and take a breather from our speculating.

"We'll see what Harbormaster Tuck thinks," I say.

"There's one more unusual thing," says Ames, rewinding the video. "Look it, I think it's something like merfolk in the shadows swimming behind Bruce and they're directing him."

Somehow it isn't too much for me on this day. Merfolk directing Bruce like they're half- human, half-fish Spielbergs.

Okay. Bruce.

*

Falmouth Police Sgt. Stan "I Don't Give A" Tuck was pushed into the role of harbormaster after he became "overzealous" during a student disciplinary incident aka "melee" at the high school. Harbormaster was a pretty safe spot for him to ease into his pension since he spent all of his free time on his own boat, mostly drunk. A drunk overseeing drunken recreational boaters. Just perfect. He sets quite an example for the town's youth.

I want to offer him a beer as we all sit on the back porch looking at the drone video but I don't want to tempt him. So we're drinking lemonade.

"I've never seen one that big. And I've been on the water since a kid. Back in the 70s, you could swim anywhere. There were no great whites in these waters. Protecting the seals brought them to us. Now they're everywhere and e-nor-mous. The fishing industry's gone after the seals gobbled all the fish. I guess we'll have to close the beaches for Labor Day weekend. Well, at least the tourist season is about over. Good thing it isn't Fourth of July. No biggie," he says. He's talkative, even without a beer in him.

"We're going to need you two in this jurisdiction for a while," Sgt. Tuck says as he hitches his belt.

I look at Ames and she at me. "How long?" I ask, trying to hold back hope.

"I don't know. At least through the end of great white season."

"How long is that?"

"By the end of October, they're starting to migrate south," Ames chimes in, jumping back into research mode.

Sgt. Tuck looks her over again. "Yeah. That's about right. Halloween. You, young lady can be very helpful with research. We don't really have the budget for it in my department of one."

Or the aptitude, I think. But I get the sense for the first time in a long time Sgt. Tuck gives a shit. He's got a new purpose before he floats off into the sunset, retirement.

And he's on our side. Because Ames will be staying at least until November. Per order of the harbormaster.

There's nothing Marie can say about that. Ames will be with me, doing what she loves to do. She can keep up with school remotely; she's so smart she's three lessons ahead anyway.

And Sgt. Tuck, he's going to need a bigger boat to replace his flimsy Boston Whaler as we all figure out exactly how this great white or whatever it is got so damn big, gorging on horsehead seals and Tremblay or whoever. Whatever it is, we'll also need to identify the merfolk who may be directing Bruce.

Squinting at Tuck, I see a bit of Robert Shaw in him. *It* was *Shaw, right?* I start to sing to myself: *Stick him in a scupper with a hosepipe bottom. Early in the morning!*

It will be such an adventure. But best of all, Ames will be staying for a while longer.

POEM OF THE MONTH

WINNERS AND HONORABLE MENTIONS OF LIT SHARK'S 2023 POEM OF THE MONTH CONTESTS

October 2023

Winner: Catherine Broadwall, "Ecology"

Honorable Mention: Shannon Frost Greenstein, "Just Another Poem about the Moon"

Honorable Mention: Beth Marquez, "From Lightning to the Earth"

November 2023

Winner: Shilo Niziolek, "Ekphrasis for the Salmon"

Honorable Mention: Emily Kerlin, "My Dentist Diagnosed Geographic Tongue and I Don't Know What That Is But I Think It Means It Wants to Talk about How We Used to Travel the World"

December 2023-January 2024

Winner: Sandra Noel, "Bioluminescence Flashes in the Pull"

Honorable Mention: Victoria M. Johnson, "How to Buy a Toilet"

Honorable Mention: Doug Van Hooser, "An Octopus Hug"

CATHERINE BROADWALL

ECOLOGY

Having trained myself on poison,
the melon tastes especially sweet,

pinned with bright tines to the
good dishes. Soft fruit oozing

its creamsicle juice. Sky that
reflects in its puddle.

Everything sugared and miracle
light. Wind hardly rattling

the table. I want to be a wife.
I want to be an artist. I hope

these impulses
are not a contradiction,

will not quarrel like
territorial foxes

chancing an encounter
in a wood.

To wife: to comb out
the snarls of life (?). To write:

to roll down a grass hill (?).
I want to be smooth. I want

to be rough. I want to be
moonlight and shelter.

And what is the natural enemy of
the woman who wants to do both?

My heart pumps blood into
my seesaw head

until all of my hair
is fire-red.

SHANNON FROST GREENSTEIN

JUST ANOTHER POEM ABOUT THE MOON

I wanted to write a happy poem,
but is that an oxymoron?
After all, I don't really have much to say
about things like the moon.
A glimmering orb, brimming with radiance, pregnant with
sunlight, leading me through the darkness like a prophet just
descended from some heavenly heights, its beauty imbuing me
with hope for the future of humanity and I smile, grateful I am
alive for another night to bear witness.

I have a lot to say about trauma
and the injustice of mental illness;
but this is a happy poem
and I'm guessing there needs to be
flowers or something.
A spectrum, a rainbow, a palette of Crayola-infused shades,
splashes of color in neon and matte, hues of magenta and
chartreuse and indigo and green, wildflowers dotting the rolling
fields as far as the eye can see, and I lay in the grass among the
blossoms, glad for the sun on my face.

I wanted to write a happy poem
because life is actually a gift.
But I had a rough go of it
for quite some time
and I'm more accustomed to writing about pain.
Happiness like a promise, like a present, like a dream; happiness

like something elusive, happiness like something reserved for everyone else. Decades of struggle to build a life worth living, bare hands constructing a new self from the ruins of CPTSD, and now that I've found happiness, is it any wonder I don't fully trust it to stay?

Now I have a family
and a temperamental cat;
Now I know the value of contentment
because I have endured life without it.
My children, my light, my redemption, my worth, compelling me like a quest to seek out light in this damaged world, rousing me to provide for them a childhood of value, playing on the floor as the cat, an asshole, a reason to smile, purrs from the depths of my lap, and I take a moment to reflect on evolution and joy; I take a moment to reflect on gratitude.

I wanted to write a happy poem
that has nothing to do with the moon;
but when I finally found serenity –
among the moon and the flowers and the children and the cat,
among the remnants and the struggle and the progress and
    the growth –
I was just unabashedly gleeful
to have even discovered happiness at all.
So I guess this did turn out to be just another poem about
    the moon, after all.

BETH MARQUEZ

FROM LIGHTNING TO THE EARTH

My magnetic other, veins to the blood
of me. Heart I am honored to beat,
I am the light stretched thin around
you. I find you 44 times a second,

our far-flung speed our wild communion,
a rhythm that none but perhaps some gods
can follow. I seek you in a kind of madness,
as though there is some part of me buried

in you that I always, always fail to find and yet
I still thrill in the seeking. My thunder calling
my percussive 'yes'–the air my throat, your
throat. I reach into your soft thighs of sand,

your shoulders and knees of rock
and you sometimes fuse my image there, holding
the photograph of my finger in crystal. You–fulsome
bride, shameless queen of my white fire.

Let us go to the lake again.
Let us blind the blushing world.

SHILO NIZIOLEK

EKPHRASIS FOR THE SALMON

> *"Dearly beloved, we are gathered here together today to look into the face of the river."*
> —Mary Ruefle

Whenever a friend goes walking, she stumbles, eyes wide, upon the uninhabited body of a wild thing. She wrote a story, never love a wild thing, and when I told her I wrote an essay that said, "I've always loved a wild thing," she said "Of course you did." And I am still trying to puzzle out what that means, but never mind that here, all you need to know is yes, I was jealous of her finding the dead, yes, I am a unwild thing and I need love. Yes, I went into the drenched-gray of the woods hoping to see the dead, ghost or holy being, it didn't matter to me. The hush that fell over me when I spotted her, tuckered out from that long and arduous swim upstream, like a body in illness. The constant hum-thrum-pushing up off the couch, body sidling between the rocks. And didn't I know, shouldn't I have known how sharp the teeth would be on a creature like that who has to spend her last moments fighting? I couldn't touch teeth, the mouth agape, barely there in the river, her face the face of the river, her eyes held no terror only purity of purpose, such singularity in her form, nearly as long as my leg. And didn't I imagine how earlier this summer, my body floated, dived, divested of the earth for a few moments to feel fluid like the salmon in the beating sun? How I shivered now, out here in the rain, looking into the face of the river like Mary Ruefle told me to, my pants getting soaked the longer I crouched toward her face in wonder, the more I imagine the brush of her body against my leg, my legs salmon-finned and thrashing. I left her to decay, to be eaten by the crows as we all end up, but here is her love letter; I wrote it just for me. You know how it is, when you are all salmon, the hunger in you shark-toothed hang-nailed effervescent. You're all smoke now, all mist hanging over the river in late November. Your scales sludge off, become part of the silt. Dear Salmon, we are gathered here together today. Dear Salmon, this is the pacific northwest, where you used to thrive, you are the moss and the ferns and the bark of the trees. Dear Salmon, I am sorry for the hunger in us. I am sorry for the take and take and take with no stand still, no long and grateful pause. I am sorry Salmon, for what is lost, that we no longer see our faces in you, the river.

EMILY KERLIN

MY DENTIST DIAGNOSED GEOGRAPHIC TONGUE AND I DON'T KNOW WHAT THAT IS BUT I THINK IT MEANS IT WANTS TO TALK ABOUT HOW WE USED TO TRAVEL THE WORLD.

my tongue licks
white icing off
Dover's cliffs
washes it down with
Black Sea
cold brew

my tongue disembarks in
Prague then complains in
perfect Czech of a chatterbox
seatmate to no one in
particular

my tongue prefers
fufu hot, follows a
chef to Kinshasa, sits
alone in a small cafe

my tongue traipses
Appalachian trails,
wears through lug
soles, knows to drink

the water from the
source

my tongue takes
pickaxe to rock in the
Kalymnos applies
chalk for friction,
bags another peak

my tongue tells about the
mangrove in Honiara that
sat like a meditating monk
ankle deep in
dark water

my tongue pulls at my
sleeve, leads us to the last
plank of a long dock,
halyards slapping under
Southern Cross

look, tongue hisses, is there
anything more important than
where we have been, what we
have seen, all we have tasted?

SANDRA NOEL

BIOLUMINESCENCE FLASHES IN THE PULL

where blackened sea sleeps.
We wait at low water's lace
for the fullness of moon
to release its tide hold.

Racing the hurrying hairline
we swag up the bay in shadow-light.
Liquid silver licks into corners,
quickens over night-white sand.

Salten spray spins its witchery.
I swim under the cellophane skin,
a trail of clothes left in silk dark.
The sea raises all boats.

VICTORIA M. JOHNSON

HOW TO BUY A TOILET

A *soft-close seat* means the lid is silent when it closes.
The neighbors hear banging doors and crashing dishes,
why put them through slamming toilet seats, too?

Comfort height means the toilet is taller than standard.
All your life you bent over,
why crouch every time you use the head?

Elongated front means there's more space to sit.
You're already crammed into a waste of a marriage,
why feel wedged-in when you relieve yourself?

Self-cleaning means shit has no place to hide
and the toilet cleans itself at the push of a button.
Unlike your spouse who has excrement hidden everywhere
and every scant utterance from you pushes his buttons.

Disposal included means the plumber takes your old toilet
for no additional fee.
Aren't you hanging onto enough useless things?
Let someone take a chunk of crap off your hands.

Eco-flush means you conserve the planet's water supply
and help keep the oceans toxic free.

You know all about toxic.
Press 1 if you pee
Press 2 if you poop
Press 3 if you want out of this shitshow

Warranty and Return Policy means you're not stuck
with something that doesn't work.
If only, if only.

DOUG VAN HOOSER

AN OCTOPUS HUG

I am empty.
It's four-thirty in the afternoon,
My thoughts are cut out paper dolls
that unfold accordion style.
Why am I thinking
of you? Every day I commute
over the same tracks, in the same seat,
no one next me.
I should move on.
Board a train in the opposite direction.
Spin a cocoon, pupate, emerge, gather
the breeze under new wings,
sally through the air.
But no. Water spreads a gas fueled fire.
A ravenous appetite steers me.
Ineffable. Ridiculous.
Addictive.
I chew on you like a wad of gum,
but you never lose taste.
I sink in the moat
I've dug around you.
Drown in limerence.

THANK YOU FOR READING

ACKNOWLEDGMENTS

Thank you to the publications in which some of these works previously appeared. We appreciate your hard work in getting these pieces out into the world, and we're thrilled to have had the opportunity to share them again.

These entries are organized in the order in which they appear in Lit Shark's Best Of 2023 Anthology:

"Meditation: Galápagos Seas" by Lorraine Caputo first appeared in her chapbook, Galápagos Shores (dancing girl press, 2019) and was reprinted in *Poetry & Places* (February 2021).

"Smiddy" by Patrick Druggan was first published in *Dreich*, Issue 8 (Season 7).

"Shearwater" by Patrick Druggan was first read at Chester Poets in July 2021.

"Driftwood Dryad" by Carol Edwards was first published in *The Ocean Waves* (Red Penguin Books, 2021) and reprinted in *Beyond the Sand and Sea* (Southern Arizona Press, 2023).

"52 Blue" and "the kind of blue" by Alyssa Harmon both appeared in Alyssa's second poetry collection, *Treading Water* (2023).

"Whale Watching Spoken Here" by Carolyn Martin first appeared in Carolyn's collection, *Finding Compass* (Queen of Wands Press, 2011).

"On Finding a Dead Deer in My Backyard" by Nolo Segundo first appeared in *Torrid Literary Journal* (2021) and was reprinted in *Lothlorien Poetry Journal*, Volume 19 (2023).

"Gamble at the Ramble" by Carol Lynn Stevenson Grellas appeared in *Lit Shark Magazine*, followed by her collection, *A Shared and Sacred Space* (Kelsay Books, 2024) before appearing in this anthology.

"Transcendence" by Edward Ahern first appeared in *Bewildering Stories*, Issue 493 (September 2012).

ABOUT OUR CONTRIBUTORS

EDWARD AHERN–he/him–Fiction
Ed Ahern resumed writing after forty odd years in foreign intelligence and international sales. He's had over 450 stories and poems published so far, and ten books. Ed works the other side of writing at *Bewildering Stories* where he manages a posse of eight review editors, and as lead editor at *Scribes Microfiction*.

GLEN ARMSTRONG–he/him–Poetry
Glen Armstrong (he/him) holds an MFA in English from the University of Massachusetts, Amherst and edits a poetry journal called *Cruel Garters*. His latest book is *Night School: Selected Early Poems*.

KB BALLENTINE—she/her—Poetry

KB Ballentine's eighth collection, *Spirit of Wild*, launched in March with Blue Light Press. Her earlier books can be found with Iris Press, Blue Light Press, Middle Creek Publishing, and Celtic Cat Publishing. Published in *North Dakota Quarterly*, *Atlanta Review,* and *Haight-Ashbury Literary Journal*, and others, her work also appears in anthologies including *I Heard a Cardinal Sing* (2022), *The Strategic Poet* (2021), *Pandemic Evolution* (2021), and *Carrying the Branch: Poets in Search of Peace* (2017). Learn more at www.kbballentine.com.

MAGGIE BAYNE—she/her—Fiction

Maggie Bayne is a fiction writer who lives in upstate New York. Her lifelong hobby of writing has shifted to a more serious pursuit since retirement. A dedicated fan of the short story, she has found that a well-crafted adventure rarely needs more than 3,500 words to grab and satisfy the readers. She has had the following published: "The Blizzard" in *October Hill Magazine*, Winter 2022, Vol. 6, Issue 4; "Rescuing Addie Stiles" in *Remington Review*, Spring 2023; "Gourmet Delight" in *ASP Literary Journal #9*, July 8, 2023; "The Return" in *Lit Shark Magazine*, Issue 2, October 2023; "Candy!" published in *Lit Shark Magazine*, Issue 3, The Spooky (TEETH) Edition, October 2023; "The Self-Reliant Woman" in *Lit Shark Magazine*, Issue 4; and "The Christmas Wish" published in *October Hill Magazine*, Winter 2023, January 2024; and "Time for a Change" to be published in *Mobius Blvd*, Issue 4, April 2024.

JANET BOWDAN–she/her–Poetry

Janet Bowdan's poems have appeared in *APR, Denver Quarterly, The Rewilding Anthology, Sequestrum, Anacapa Review* and elsewhere. The editor of *Common Ground Review*, she teaches at Western New England University and lives in Northampton, Massachusetts, with her husband, their son, and a book-nibbling chinchilla.

CATHERINE BROADWALL–she/her–Poetry

Catherine Broadwall is the author of *Water Spell* (Cornerstone Press, forthcoming 2025), *Fulgurite* (Cornerstone Press, 2023), *Shelter in Place* (Spuyten Duyvil, 2019), and other collections. Her writing has appeared in *Bellingham Review, Colorado Review, Mid-American Review*, and other journals. She was the winner of the 2019-2020 COG Poetry Award and a finalist for the 2021 Mississippi Review Prize in poetry. She is an assistant professor at DigiPen Institute of Technology, where she teaches creative writing and literature. Her website is www.catherinebroadwall.com.

LORRAINE CAPUTO–she/her–Poetry

Wandering troubadour Lorraine Caputo is a documentary poet, translator and travel writer. Her works appear in over 400 journals on six continents; and 23 collections of poetry –including *In the Jaguar Valley* (dancing girl press, 2023) and *Caribbean Interludes* (Origami Poems Project, 2022). She also authors travel narratives, articles, and guidebooks. Her writing has been honored by the Parliamentary Poet Laureate of Canada (2011), and nominated for the Best of the Net and the Pushcart Prize. Caputo has done literary readings from Alaska to the Patagonia. She journeys through Latin America with her faithful knapsack Rocinante, listening to the voices of the pueblos and Earth.

TRICIA CASEY–she/her–Nonfiction

Tricia Casey is a non-profit and higher education consultant who advises clients on fundraising, strategic planning, communications, and operations. She lives in southern New Hampshire but grew up in Hawaii. Story telling has featured heavily throughout her life and began around the fires at Girl Scout camp and at the heels of an Irish-American family whose real-life experiences, especially the sad ones, were always presented with humor and irony.

ALAN COHEN–he/him–Poetry

Alan Cohen's first publication as a poet was in the PTA Newsletter when he was 10 years old. Vassar College (with a BA in English) and University of California at Davis Medical School, did his internship in Boston and his residency in Hawaii, and was then a Primary Care physician, teacher, and Chief of Primary Care at the VA, first in Fresno, CA and later in Roseburg, OR. He now lives with his wife of 44 years in Eugene, OR.

MARK CONNORS–he/him–Poetry

Mark Connors is a widely published poet from Leeds. His debut, *Life is a Long Song*, was published by OWF Press in 2015. *Nothing is Meant to be Broken* was published by Stairwell Books in 2017. *Optics* was published by YAFFLE in 2019. *After* was published by YAFFLE in 2021. Find more at www.markconnors.co.uk. He is a managing editor and co-founder of Yaffle Press and Yaffle's Nest.

DALE E. COTTINGHAM–he/him–Poetry

Dale Cottingham has published poems and reviews of poetry collections in many journals, including *Prairie Schooner*, *Ashville Poetry Review*, and *Rain Taxi*. He is a Pushcart Nominee, a Best of Net Nominee, the winner of the 2019 New Millennium Award for Poem of the Year, and was a finalist in the 2022 Great Midwest Poetry Contest. His debut volume of poems, *Midwest Hymns*, launched in April, 2023. He lives in Edmond, Oklahoma.

PATRICK DRUGGAN–he/him–Poetry

Patrick grew up in Glasgow and went to university there. He is a scientist and has worked on diagnostic tests for cancers and infections on and off for the past 35 years. He is dyslexic. He learned to write poetry when no-one was looking. He has been published in *Dreich*, *Culture Matters*, *Black Nore*, the Full Circle Anthology of Chester Poets, and in Yaffle Press' Whirlagust IV.

CAROL EDWARDS–she/her–Poetry

Carol Edwards is a northern California native transplanted to southern Arizona. She grew up reading fantasy and classic novels, climbing trees, and acquiring frequent grass stains. She currently enjoys a coffee addiction and raising her succulent army. Her favorite shark is the whale shark.

Her poetry has been published in numerous publications, both online and print, including *Space and Time*, *POETiCA REViEW*, *The Post Grad Journal*, *The Wild Word*, *Written Tales Magazine*, and *Lit Shark Magazine*, and in anthologies from White Stag Publishing,

Southern Arizona Press, Red Penguin Books, The Ravens Quoth Press, and Black Spot Books. More of her work is forthcoming in *Playlist of the Damned* (Weird Little Worlds), *Mother Knows Best* (Black Spot Books), *Frisson* (The Ravens Quoth Press), and *About Time* (Red Penguin Books).

Her debut poetry collection, *The World Eats Love*, released April 25, 2023 from The Ravens Quoth Press. You can follow her on Instagram @practicallypoetical, and on X/Twitter and Facebook @practicallypoet. Her website is www.practicallypoetical.wordpress.com.

MICHAEL FLANAGAN–he/him–Poetry
Mike Flanagan lives in Minnesota with Lady, his mutt of dubious lineage. He fly fishes with no great skill but believes that walking with Lady, fly fishing, and writing short poetry keep him going.

ANNETTE GAGLIARDI–she/her–Poetry
Annette Gagliardi looks at the dimly tinted shadows and morphed illusions that becomes life and finds illumination. She sees what others do not and grasps the fruit hiding there, then squeezes all the juice that life has to offer and serves it up as poetry–or jelly, depending on the day. Her work has appeared in many literary journals in Canada, England, and the USA, including *Motherwell, St. Paul Almanac, Wisconsin Review, American Diversity Report, Origami Poems Project, Amethyst Review, Door Is A Jar, Trouble Among the Stars, Sylvia Magazine, Lit Shark Magazine*, and others. Gagliardi's first poetry collection, *A Short*

Supply of Viability, and her first historical fiction, *Ponderosa Pines: Days of the Deadwood Forest Fire*, were both published in 2022, the latter which won the PenCraft Book Award for Fall, 2023. Find more at www.annette-gagliardi.com

J.D. GEVRY–they/them–Poetry

J.D. Gevry, MPH, is an emerging poet whose writing is influenced by their experiences living at the intersection of a variety of identities, a deep love of nature, and queer polyamorous life. Their work has appeared in *The Bitchin' Kitsch*, *Lit Shark Magazine*, Querencia Press's *Summer 2023 Anthology*, and *just femme and dandy*, among others, and was longlisted for the 2023 erbacce-prize.

GTIMOTHY GORDON–he/him–Poetry

Gordon's *Dream Wind* was published 2020 (Spirit-of-the-Ram) and *Ground of This Blue Earth* (Mellen), while *Everything Speaking Chinese* received RIVERSTONE P Poetry Prize (AZ). Work appears in *AGNI*, *American Literary Review*, *Cincinnati Poetry Review*, *Mississippi Review*, *New York Quarterly*, *Phoebe*, *RHINO*, *Sonora Review*, *Texas Observer*, several nominated for Pushcarts. His eighth book, *Empty*, was published 04 January 2024 (Cyberwit P), and *Blue Business* is in-progress.

SHANNON FROST GREENSTEIN–she/her–Poetry

Shannon Frost Greenstein resides in Philadelphia with her children and soulmate. She is the author of *The Wendigo of Wall Street*, a novella forthcoming with *Emerge Literary Journal*. Shannon is a former Ph.D. candidate in Continental Philosophy and a multi-

Pushcart Prize nominee. Her work has appeared in *McSweeney's, Internet Tendency, Pithead, Chapel, WAS Quarterly, Bending Genres*, and elsewhere. Shannon was recently a finalist for the 2023 Ohio State University Press Journal Non/Fiction Prize. Follow her on her website at shannonfrostgreenstein.com

ALYSSA HARMON—she/her—Poetry

Alyssa Harmon earned her master's in creative writing from the University of West Florida. She has dozens of publications, including two published poetry books: *treading water* is her second poetry collection; *seven years* is her first. She has plans for even more books, drawing on her life experiences to share with the world. When she's not writing poetry, you can find her reading a good book, swimming laps in the pool, or traveling to new countries.

MATT HENRY—he/him—Poetry

2017 Graduate of Indiana University, Master of Arts in English. Likes ice hockey, guitar, writing/reading poetry, and video games. Dislikes cockroaches and dust mites.

KEITH HOERNER—he/him—Fiction

Keith Hoerner (BS, MFA, current PhD student) is founding editor of the Microlit ezine *The Dribble Drabble Review*, a Webby Award recognized cultural website. His work has been featured in 150+ lit mags and anthologies across five continents. *Splish. Splash.*

MICHAEL LEE JOHNSON–he/him–POETRY

Michael Lee Johnson lived ten years in Canada during the Vietnam era. Today he is a poet in the greater Chicagoland area, IL. He has over 296 YouTube poetry videos. Johnson is an internationally published poet in 44 countries, has several published poetry books, has been nominated for 6 Pushcart Prize awards, and 6 Best of the Net nominations. He is editor-in-chief of 3 poetry anthologies, all available on Amazon, and has several poetry books and chapbooks. He has over 453 published poems. Michael is the administrator of 6 Facebook Poetry groups. Member Illinois State Poetry Society: http://www.illinoispoets.org/.

VICTORIA M. JOHNSON–she/her–Poetry

Victoria M. Johnson is the author of four books and two mini books. Her poetry, memoir, and flash stories appear in online literary journals and print anthologies. When she is not writing, Victoria is a reiki master, meditation teacher, zumba instructor, and writing coach. Victoria is the founder of Creative Breath, a supportive and enriching place for writers.

EMILY KERLIN–she/her–Poetry

Emily Kerlin has published poems in journals such as *Cider Press Review*, *Sheila-Na-Gig*, *Blue Mountain Review*, *Storm Cellar*, *Split Rock Review* and the *MacGuffin*. Her book, *Twenty-One Farewells*, won Minerva Rising's 2023 chapbook contest. She lives with her family in Urbana, Illinois where she teaches the difference between "chicken" and "kitchen" to English learners. Find her at emilykerlin.com

DEBORAH KERNER–she/her–Poetry

Deborah Kerner is a poet and an artist living in Ojai, California. Her poems have appeared in many poetry journals such as *Rabid Oak, Mad Swirl,* and *Synchronized Chaos.* She shares a modest house with her husband, Richard, who is also an artist. She lived and taught in India. Over many years, her travels to various places in the world have deepened an all-embracing vision of being alive on a radiant planet. Deborah and her husband facilitate week-long retreats for the Krishnamurti Center in Ojai, focusing on the potential for a transformation of human consciousness. A selection of Deborah's poems and art can be seen on her website: deborah-kerner.com

HELGA KIDDER–she/her–Poetry

Helga Kidder lives in the Tennessee hills with her husband. She loves to look on nature and find the connection to her surroundings. Her poems have recently been published in *Bloodroot, Salvation South, Kakalak,* and others. She has five collections of poetry. Her fifth collection, *Learning Curve,* includes poems about immigration and assimilation.

CRAIG R. KIRCHNER–he/him–Poetry

Craig Kirchner thinks of poetry as hobo art. He loves storytelling and the aesthetics of the paper and pen. He has had two poems nominated for the Pushcart, and has a book of poetry, *Roomful of Navels.* After a writing hiatus, he was recently published in *Decadent Review, New World Writing, Wild Violet, Ink in Thirds, Last Leaves, Literary Heist, Quail Bell, The Globe Review, Ariel Chart, Lit Shark Magazine,* and has work forthcoming in *Cape Magazine, Flora Fiction,*

Young Ravens Literary Review, Chiron Review, and several dozen other journals.

ASHLEY KNOWLTON–she/her–Poetry

Ashley Knowlton teaches English and writes poetry for enjoyment. Her work has been published in *Pomona Valley Review, DASH, Abandoned Mine, Cobra Lily, Trajectory, Mom Egg Review Online Quarterly, Evening Street Review, Neologism Poetry Journal,* and *The Waiting Room.* She lives in northern California with her spouse, sons, and their many animals.

H.K.G. LOWERY–he/him–Poetry

H. K. G. Lowery is a writer & musician from Gateshead, United Kingdom. He gained a Distinction in his Masters degree in Creative Writing from Graduate College, Lancaster University, where he worked with Paul Muldoon, Paul Farley & Terry Eagleton. The Department of English Literature & Creative Writing awarded him with the 2021/2022 Portfolio Prize for his "outstanding performance" as highest-achiever in The Faculty of Arts and Social Sciences. Lowery has been shortlisted for The Bedford International Award & The Terry Kelly Poetry Prize, & longlisted for The Fiction Factory Flash Competition. His publications include: *An Enquiry into the Delight of Existence and the Sublime* (Austin Macauley Publishers, 2020), *Being and Becoming* (Kindle Direct Publishing, 2021), *Death, And Other Angels* (Errant, 2022), *9:45 Drama* (Kindle Direct Publishing, 2022) & *Moonflowers* (Aurum Journal, 2023). To date, Lowery has been published in: *Poetry Salzburg, Amsterdam Quarterly, Pennine Platform, Obsessed With Pipework, Publishers Weekly, Hyacinth Review, The Ofi Press, Hearth & Coffin, StepAway*

Magazine, Dreich Magazine, Granny's Tea Poetry Magazine, Train River Publishing, Sylvia Magazine, Patchwork, Wildfire Words, Lancaster Flash & Disabled Tales.

JENNIFER MACBAIN-STEPHENS–she/her– Poetry

Jennifer MacBain-Stephens went to NYU's Tisch School of the Arts and now lives in Iowa where she is landlocked. Her fifth, full length poetry collection, *Pool Parties*, is now available from Unsolicited Press. She is the author of fifteen chapbooks. Some of her work appears in *The Pinch*, *South Broadway Ghost Society*, *Cleaver*, *Dream Pop*, *Slant*, *Yalobusha Review*, and *Grist*. She is a member of the Iowa City Poetry Council and the director of the monthly reading series, *Today You are Perfect*, sponsored by the non-profit Iowa City Poetry. Find her online at http://jennifermacbainstephens.com/.

BETH MARQUEZ–she/her–Poetry

Beth Marquez has recent or upcoming publications in *Cathexis*, *October Hill*, *Spillway*, and the *Like a Girl* anthology from Lucid Moose Press, which nominated her poem, "Shedding," for a Pushcart Prize. She is a 2017 Pink Door Fellow and holds three mathematics degrees. She is a freelance statistician, poet, and singer-songwriter residing in Altadena, California.

CAROLYN MARTIN–she/her–Poetry

Blissfully retired in Clackamas, Oregon, Carolyn Martin is a lover of gardening and snorkeling, feral cats and backyard birds, writing, and photography. Since the only poem she wrote in high school was red-penciled "extremely maudlin," she is amazed she has continued to write. Her poems have appeared in more than 175 journals throughout North America, Australia, and the UK, and her latest collection, *It's in the Cards*, was just released by Kelsay Books. See more at www.carolynmartinpoet.com

BETH MATHISON–she/her–Poetry and Fiction
Beth Mathison has work published in *The Foliate Oak* (including the 2008 and 2009 annual "Best Of" print editions), *Haiku Journal*, 365 Tomorrows. com, MysteryAuthors.com, *Drops of Crimson*, *Colored Chalk*, and *The Citron Review*. Stories published with Untreed Reads include *Mobsters for the Holidays; Criminally Hilarious Short Stories* (also an audio book) and the short story romance series, *Young at Heart*. Her poem "My Grandmother's Hands" was featured in *Verse Wisconsin*, along with a reading with Wisconsin's first Poet Laureate (Ellen Kort). Beth lives with her family in the Upper Midwest, and during the cold winter months, she dreams of snorkeling in the Riviera Maya.

URSULA MCCABE URSULA–she/her–Poetry
Ursula McCabe lives in Portland Oregon where the ocean is not too far away. Her poet father, Robert Huff taught at Western Washington State University until his death in 1993. Ursula's poems can be seen in *Piker Press*, *Bluebird World*, *The Ekphrastic Review*, *Lit Shark Magazine*, The Wee Sparrow Poetry Press, and other places.

LAUREN K. NIXON–she/her–Poetry
An ex-archaeologist who swapped the past for the present, Lauren K. Nixon is the author of numerous short stories, *The Fox and the Fool*, *Mayflies*, *The Last Human Getaway,* and *The House of Vines*, along with poetry collections (including *Wild Daughter*, *Marry Your*

Chameleon, and *umbel.*). She has also written two plays – one even on purpose!

Her poems appear in *Rhubarb: Seconds*, *Lit Shark Magazine*, *Ekphrastic Review*, *The Lake*, *Apricot Press*, *Dream Catcher*, *Reach*, *The Dawntreader*, and *The Black Nore Review*, along with several collections by *The Superstars*.

When she's not writing, she can be found pootling around the garden or library, researching weird stuff, making miniatures, annoying the cats, and playing board games. You can find out more at her website: www.laurenknixon.com

SHILO NIZIOLEK – she/her – Poetry
Shilo Niziolek has written *Fever* and *atrophy* (Querencia Press), *Porcelain Ghosts* forthcoming from Querencia Press, *A Thousand Winters In Me* (Gasher Press), *I Am Not An Erosion: Poems Against Decay* (Ghost City Press), and Dirt Eaters (Bottlecap Press). Her work has appeared in *Juked, Honey Literary, West Trade Review, Entropy, Pork Belly Press*, and *Phoebe Journal,* among others. Shilo is a writing instructor at Clackamas Community College, a workshop facilitator for the Literary Arts, and is the editor and co-founder of the literary magazine, *Scavengers*. Find her on Instagram @shiloniziolek

SANDRA NOEL – she/her – Poetry
Sandra Noel is a poet from Jersey, Channel Islands. She enjoys writing about the ordinary in unusual ways, her passion for sea swimming and her love of nature often weaving its way through her work. Sandra has poems featured online and print magazines and anthologies. Over the past year she has been longlisted, shortlisted and

highly commended in various competitions. She has poems on buses in Guernsey from the Guernsey International Poetry Competition 2022 and 2023. Sandra is finalising her first collection which will be published by Yaffle Press in 2024.

JESS L. PARKER–she/her–Poetry

Jess L Parker is a poet and strategist from the Upper Peninsula of Michigan. Jess lives in Fitchburg, WI., with her husband and two-year-old son. Her debut poetry collection, *Star Things*, won the 2020 Dynamo Verlag Book Prize. Jess' poems have appeared in *Bramble*, *Kosmos Quarterly*, *Blue Heron Review*, and elsewhere. Jess holds a B.A. of English and Spanish from Northern Michigan University, an M.A. of Spanish Literature from UW-Madison, and an MBA.

NANCY MACHLIS RECHTMAN–she/her–Poetry and Fiction

Nancy Machlis Rechtman has had poetry and short stories published in *Your Daily Poem*, *Writing In A Woman's Voice*, *Grande Dame*, *Impspired*, *Paper Dragon*, *Fresh Words*, *The Writing Disorder*, *Young Ravens Literary Review*, and more. She wrote freelance Lifestyle stories for a local newspaper, and she was the copy editor for another paper. She writes a blog called *Inanities* at https://nancywriteon.wordpress.com.

RUSSELL RICHARDSON—he/him—Fiction

Russell Richardson is lead editor and site manager at postingandtoasting.com, a New York Knicks community. When not writing about the Knicks or working as a professional freelancer, he writes short stories, illustrates, and creates children's books to benefit kids with cancer. His YA novel, *Level Up and Die!*, and a short story collection, *Nocturnal Medley: Fourteen Weird Tales,* are available at Amazon. He resides in Binghamton, NY., with his wife and sons.

RIE SHERIDAN ROSE—she/her—Poetry and Fiction

Rie Sheridan Rose multitasks. A lot. Her short stories appear in numerous anthologies, including *Nightmare Stalkers and Dream Walkers: Vols 1 and 2*, and *Killing It Softly*. She has authored twelve novels, six poetry chapbooks, and lyrics for dozens of songs. Find more info on www.riewriter.com.

CASSANDRA O'SULLIVAN SACHAR—she/her—Fiction and Nonfiction

Cassandra O'Sullivan Sachar is a writer and associate English professor in Pennsylvania. Her creative work has appeared in over forty publications, including *The Dillydoun Review*, *Quagmire Literary Magazine*, *Wyldblood Magazine*, *The Horror Zine*, and *Tales from the Moonlit Path*. She holds a Doctorate of Education with a Literacy Specialization from the University of Delaware and an MFA in Creative Writing from Wilkes University. Her novel, *Darkness There but Something More* (Wicked House Publishing), and short horror story collection, *Keeper of Corpses and*

Other Dark Tales (Velox Books), will both be published in 2024. Read her work at cassandraosullivansachar.com.

JOEL SAVISHINSKY–he/him–Poetry

Joel Savishinsky is a retired gerontologist and environmental anthropologist. His books include *The Trail of The Hare: Life and Stress in An Arctic Community* and *Breaking the Watch: The Meanings of Retirement in America*; the latter won the Gerontological Society of America's Kalish Award, its book-of-the-year prize. A Pushcart Prize nominee, and California State Poetry Society and Cirque Journal award winner, his poetry, fiction and essays have appeared in *Atlanta Review, Beyond Words, California Quarterly, Cirque Journal, The Examined Life Journal, The New York Times, Poetry Quarterly, SLANT,* and *Windfall.* In 2023, The Poetry Box published his collection, *Our Aching Bones, Our Breaking Hearts: Poems on Aging.* He lives in Seattle, helping to raise his five grandchildren, and considers himself a recovering academic and unrepentant activist. Find more at www.ithaca.edu/faculty/savishin

MANDY SCHIFFRIN–she/her–Poetry

Mandy Schiffrin is half-British, half-Argentinian, and lives in the Netherlands. Mandy has always had a passion for words, language, and how we understand what we mean by what we say. In fact, she obtained a doctorate studying this topic, in Artificial Intelligence (Natural Language Processing), and still works in the same field to this day. Mandy explores this with her poetry too, and has recently started submitting some of her work for publication. She has poems either already published, or accepted, in the following magazines and journals: *Black Nore Review*, *The Crowstep Journal*, *Ink, Sweat and Tears*, *Dawntreader*, *Obsessed with Pipework*, and *The High Window*, as well as for a couple of upcoming anthologies.

LARRY SCHUG—he/him—Poetry
Larry Schug is retired after a life of various kinds of physical labor. He is currently a volunteer writing tutor at the College of St. Benedict/St. John's University. He lives with his wife and one cat in a little house on 55 acres of permanently preserved land in St. Wendel, Twp., Minnesota. He has published eight books of poems, the latest being *A Blanket of Raven Feathers* with North Star Press. His website is www.larryschugpoet.com

NOLO SEGUNDO NOLO—he/him—Poetry
Nolo Segundo, pen name of L.j.Carber, 76, became a late blooming poet in his 8th decade in over 180 literary journals and anthologies in America, England, Canada, Romania, Scotland. China, Sweden, Australia, Portugal, India, Australia, Turkey, Hungary, Israel, and Italy. The trade publisher Cyberwit.net has released 3 poetry books: *The Enormity of Existence* [2020]; *Of Ether and Earth* [2021]; and *Soul Songs* [2022]. These titles and much of his work reflect the awareness he's had for over 50 years since having an NDE whilst almost drowning in a Vermont river: that he has--IS-- a consciousness that predates birth and survives death, what poets for millennia have called a soul.

CAROL LYNN STEVENSON GRELLAS–she/her– Poetry

Carol Lynn Stevenson Grellas is a recent graduate of Vermont College of Fine Arts, MFA in Writing program. She is the author of sixteen poetry collections, including several chapbooks. Her latest collection, *Alice in Ruby Slippers*, was short-listed for the 2021 Eric Hoffer Grand Prize and awarded an honorable mention in the Poetry category. Her work has been published or is forthcoming in some of the following journals: *The Comstock Review*, *War, Literature and the Arts*, *Redactions*, *Verse Daily*, and many more. She has served as editor-in-chief for both *The Orchards Poetry Journal* and *Tule Review*. An eleven-time Pushcart Prize nominee and seven-time Best of the Net nominee, according to family lore, she is a direct descendant of Robert Louis Stevenson.

ANNIE SULLIVAN–she/her–Poetry

Annie Sullivan is the author of three young adult novels published by an imprint of Harper Collins. They include *A Touch of Gold*, *A Curse of Gold*, and *Tiger Queen*. She is also the co-author on one of the well-known "...For Dummies" books. She grew up in Indianapolis, Indiana, and received her master's degree in Creative Writing from Butler University. She loves fairytales, everything Jane Austen, and traveling.

MARIANNE TEFFT–she/her–Poetry

Marianne Tefft is a poet who daylights as a Montessori teacher in Toronto. Her poems and short stories appear in print, online, and on air in North America, Europe, Asia and the Caribbean. She is the author of the poetry collections *Full Moon Fire: Spoken Songs of Love* and *Moonchild: Poems for Moon Lovers*.

DOUG VAN HOOSER–he/him–Poetry

Doug Van Hooser splits his time between suburban Chicago where he uses pseudonyms with baristas, and southern Wisconsin where he enjoys sculling and cycling. His poetry has appeared in numerous publications and has been nominated for the Pushcart Prize and Orison Anthology. He has also published short fiction and had readings of his plays in Chicago. His work can be found at dougvanhooser.com

STEVE ZISSON–he/him–Fiction

Steve Zisson is a biotech journalist whose fiction has appeared in *Daily Science Fiction, Nature, Little Blue Marble, Selene Quarterly, Hyphen Punk*, among other places. He also edited a science fiction/fantasy/horror anthology, *A Punk Rock Future*. He lives on the North Shore of Boston with his family near a lake that once produced great quantities of high quality ice that was exported around the world not so long ago when there was no refrigeration and the climate was colder. As far as he knows, the lake is not connected to the ocean three miles east by a creek or canal where a bull shark or great white might mistakenly swim up. Probably.

MCKENZIE LYNN TOZAN—she/her—Editor-in-Chief of *Lit Shark Magazine*

McKenzie Lynn Tozan is a formerly Midwestern writer, transplanted to coastal Croatia. She is a published poet and novelist, the Editor-in-Chief of *Lit Shark* and the *Banned Book Review*. Her poems, essays, and book reviews have been featured in *The Rumpus*, *Green Mountains Review*, *Whale Road Review*, *Rogue Agent*, *POPSUGAR*, *Motherly*, and *Encore Magazine*. Her short horror story collection, *What We Find in the Dark*, and her horror novella, *Black As Black*, are both forthcoming from The Shiver Collective in 2024. Find more at www.mckenzielynntozan.com

FIN.

(UNTIL DECEMBER 2024 FOR OUR NEXT ANTHOLOGY...)

Made in United States
Troutdale, OR
03/21/2024